STUDY GU…

Prepared by Teresa Vanderweide
Mount Royal College

CONTEMPORARY LINGUISTIC ANALYSIS

An Introduction

Sixth Edition

William O'Grady
University of Hawaii

John Archibald
University of Calgary

PEARSON
Longman
Toronto

For Chris and his girls (J, M, L, D, N . . .)

ISBN 13: 978-0-321-50281-0

ISBN 10: 0-321-50281-7

Executive Acquisitions Editor: Christine Cozens

Sponsoring Editor: Carolin Sweig

Senior Developmental Editor: Jennifer Murray

Production Editor: Avivah Wargon

Copy Editor: Jen Abel

Production Coordinator: Avinash Chandra

2 3 4 5 12 11 10 09

Printed and bound in Canada.

PEARSON
Longman

CONTENTS

PREFACE

This study guide is intended to accompany the sixth edition of *Contemporary Linguistic Analysis: An Introduction*. I began the study guide as a series of worksheets distributed to students in class. I gradually expanded these worksheets to include brief explanations of course content and additional practice exercises, and eventually linked all of this material together with reminders and review sheets. As the worksheets evolved into a study guide, they became more generic and all-encompassing, making the resulting study guide potentially of use to any instructor of introductory linguistics using *Contemporary Linguistic Analysis: An Introduction*. For the sixth edition of this textbook, I have more closely linked the study guide to the text by including references to examples found in tables, as well as references to figures diagramming important concepts (e.g., syllable structure, word trees, syntactic structure, etc.). I have also included many more general questions for students as well as short exercises, both of which are aimed at getting students to actively think about the concepts presented in the text. These features are all designed to complement the text's ability to engage students with the material.

The study guide contains a preview of major concepts (Chapter One) followed by six chapters (Chapters Two through Seven) that correspond to the core components of theoretical linguistics: phonetics, phonology, morphology, syntax, and semantics, as well as historical linguistics. While the text covers many more branches of linguistics (e.g., classification, acquisition, sociolinguistics, etc.) than does the study guide, the chapters included in the study guide correspond to the areas of introductory linguistics that students typically require a great deal of practice with in order to better understand the methods of analysis used within those particular branches of linguistics. I hope that this study guide fulfills these needs.

Each chapter in the study guide begins with a list of the main topics and/or concepts found in that chapter. The different sections found in each chapter correspond to this list. Each section contains brief explanations of important concepts and questions for students about these concepts, along with numerous exercises. All chapters include reminders of important concepts, and conclude with a review checklist that students can use to prepare for exams. All material included in the study guide has either been modified from existing worksheets, or designed specifically to enhance the content of *Contemporary Linguistic Analysis: An Introduction*.

I gratefully acknowledge contributions made by Carrie Dyck, Elaine Sorensen, Leone Sveinson, Joyce Hildebrand, and Lorna Rowsell, without whom this study guide would not have been possible. I would like to thank all the reviewers for their comments, especially Carrie Dyck and William O'Grady, whose invaluable suggestions and advice have improved the overall quality of the study guide. Thanks also go to Elizabeth Ritter for using an early version of the study guide with her students and providing valuable feedback. Finally, I extend my sincere thanks and gratitude to Michael Dobrovolsky and John Archibald for their continued support and encouragement.

CHAPTER 1. LANGUAGE: A PREVIEW

The following are some of the important concepts found in this chapter. Make sure you are familiar with them.

1. Specialization
2. Creativity
3. Linguistic Competence
4. Grammar

SPECIALIZATION

Humans are specialized for language. The characteristics below illustrate some of the aspects of our special capacity for language.

1. Speech Organs

Our lungs, vocal cords, tongue, teeth, lips, and nasal passages are used for both survival (e.g., breathing and eating), and for producing the sounds of our language.

2. Speech Perception

We are also equipped for speech perception, and we have the ability at birth. Studies have shown that newborns are able to perceive subtle differences between sounds and are even able to perceive differences between sounds they have never heard before.

3. The Human Mind

Our minds form words, build sentences, and interpret meanings in ways not found in other species.

This specialization for language sets us apart from all other creatures!

CREATIVITY

Human language is creative. That is, language does not provide us with a set of pre-packaged messages. Rather, it allows us to produce and understand new words and sentences whenever needed. However, there are limitations on both the form and interpretation of new words and sentences. Linguists attempt to identify, understand and explain these limitations.

Exercise! Think about the limitations on the creativity of language by answering the following questions.

1. Put a check mark beside those words that are possible English words.

   a. tlim ____________________
   b. stuken ____________________
   c. tseg ____________________
   d. fomp ____________________
   e. plog ____________________
   f. skpit ____________________
   g. ngan ____________________
   h. breb ____________________

   Think about why some of the above are not possible English words. (HINT: Look at the combination of sounds found at the beginning of the words.)

2. Put a check mark beside those words that are possible English words.

   a. speakless ____________________
   b. beautifulness ____________________
   c. unrug ____________________
   d. reglorify____________________
   e. horseable ____________________
   f. weedic ____________________

   Think about why some of the above are not possible English words. (HINT: Think about the prefix or suffix and its contribution to the meaning of the word.)

3. Put a check mark beside those sentences that are possible English sentences.

   a. The building is swept yesterday evening. ____________________
   b. The building is swept every morning. ____________________
   c. Every child should obey his parents. ____________________
   d. Somebody left their gloves in the theatre. ____________________
   e. George surprised Mary with a party. ____________________
   f. Joe surprised the stone. ____________________

   Think about why some of the above are not possible English sentences.

4. Now try this!

   a. Arrange the words "bird", "worm", "catches", "early", "every", "the", and "a" into an English sentence.

   b. Think of other arrangements of the same words that result in different sentences from the one you just put together.

   c. Think about how you could arrange the words so that the sentence you create is not an acceptable English sentence.

LINGUISTIC COMPETENCE

Linguistic Competence can be defined as subconscious knowledge which enables the native speakers of a language to produce and understand an unlimited number of both familiar and novel utterances. The native speakers of a language are those who have acquired it as children in a home rather than in a classroom.

Linguists divide the subconscious knowledge that the native speakers of a language share into the following fields of study:

1. Phonetics: the study of the articulation and perception of speech sounds

2. Phonology: the study of how speech sounds pattern in language

3. Morphology: the study of word structure and word formation

4. Syntax: the study of sentence structure

5. Semantics: the study of the meaning of words and sentences

This subconscious knowledge allows the speakers of a language to produce an infinite number of sentences, many of which we have never uttered or heard before. We don't memorize language: we create it.

Go back to the exercise on Creativity. For each data set, determine which aspect of your linguistic competence allows you to decide which are possible English words and sentences.

GRAMMAR

Grammar, to a linguist, refers to all the elements of our linguistic competence: phonetics, phonology, morphology, syntax, and semantics. In very general terms, grammar can be defined as the mental system of knowledge needed to form and interpret the sounds, words, and sentences of our language. The study of grammar is central to understanding language and what it means to know a language. This is because all languages have sounds, words and sentences; all grammars allow for the expression of any thought; all grammars share common principles and tendencies called universals; all grammars are equal; and all grammars change over time. However, our grammatical knowledge is subconscious: we can decide what sounds right and what does not even though we may not be sure about why this is so.

There are two perspectives on grammar: prescriptive and descriptive. A prescriptive grammar gives the socially accepted rules within a language, while a descriptive grammar is an objective description of the knowledge that native speakers share. Examine the boxes below (adapted from *The Verbal Edge*, Readers Digest, 1994) and see if you can tell which type of grammar is being exemplified.

WRONG: "Between you and I ..."
RIGHT: "Between you and me ..."

On an episode of the TV sitcom "Home Improvement", handyman Tim Taylor said of competitor Bob Vila, "A lot of people think there's a big rivalry between Bob and I."

That may sound correct, but the pronoun *I* is wrong here. *Between* is a preposition, and prepositions are always followed by objects. *I* is a subject or nominative pronoun. So are *he, she, we,* and *they*. Objective pronouns that follow a preposition are *me, you, him, her, us,* and *them*.

Use the rhyme "Between thee and me" as a reminder.

WRONG: "She is older than me."
RIGHT: "She is older than I."

Unlike *between,* the word *than* is not a preposition; it's a conjunction—a word that joins two sentence, words, or phrases. In this case there are two sentences: (1) "She is older" and (2) "I am"—but the *am* has been dropped, and that throws people off.

In a comparison joined by *than* or *as*, just complete the sentence, and the correct word will be obvious. You wouldn't say "He is smarter than me am", so it must be "He is smarter than I".

WRONG: "Who do I ask?"
RIGHT: "Whom do I ask?"

Who and *whom* will never stump you if you remember: *Who* is generally appropriate whenever you use *he, she,* or *they*; *whom* acts as a substitute for *him, her,* or *them.* Sometimes it helps to recast a question into a statement. In this example, you'd never say "I ask he", so the correct wording is "Whom do I ask?" ("But that sounds stuffy", you say. Yes—which is why the incorrect "Who do I ask?" is sometimes used in informal situations.)

WRONG: "The demand for durable goods such as cars and home appliances were unchanged last month."
RIGHT: "The demand for durable goods such as cars and home appliances was unchanged last month."

A CNN news anchor delivered this blooper, which goes to show that even professionals err. The mistake was mating a plural verb with a singular subject. And it often happens as it did here: The subject of the sentence, *demand*, was singular, but it got separated from the verb by the plural phrase *such as cars and home appliances.* Distracted by these particulars, the anchor forgot that she was speaking in the singular and used a plural verb. Keep your mind on the subject—what it is you're talking about.

The above are all examples of a prescriptivist view on language. While a prescriptivist grammar is useful in helping people learn a foreign language, in that it contains the socially accepted rules for language use, linguists are more interested in descriptive grammar.

Spot the Difference! Each of the following aspects of linguistic competence contains two statements. See if you can identify which statement is prescriptivist and which is descriptivist. Do this by writing either D.G. (Descriptive Grammar) or P.G. (Prescriptive Grammar) beside each statement.

1. Sounds

_______________ The English words ***Mary, merry***, and ***marry*** should be pronounced differently because they are spelled differently.

_______________ English contains over twenty different consonant sounds.

Think about how many different vowel sounds are found in English.

Do all languages have the same consonant and/or vowel sounds? Think of a language that has different vowel or consonant sounds from English.

2. Words

_______________ The use of ***thunk*** and not ***thought*** as the past tense of the verb ***think*** is an example of how change is causing the English language to deteriorate.

_______________ Many nouns in English are formed by adding the suffix -***ment*** to words (e.g., achievement, government, judgment).

Think about why no English speaker would construct the word ***chairment***.

3. Sentences

_______________ There are at least two ways in English to make a sentence refer to the future.

_______________ The auxiliary ***will*** should be used with the 3rd person singular (i.e., *he, she, it*), whereas ***shall*** should be used for all other persons (e.g., He will go, but we shall stay.).

Think of two different ways to change the sentence ***The horses eat hay.*** to refer to the future.

Think about how other languages make statements refer to future time.

4. Meaning

_______________ The word ***cool*** should only be used to refer to temperature.

_______________ Many words in a language often have opposite meanings (e.g., hot/cold, light/dark).

Think about how the meaning of a sentence is different from the meaning of the words that comprise it.

QUICK REMINDER!

Linguistics is the study of the structure of human language, and linguists attempt to describe and explain, in an objective and non-judgmental fashion, the internalized and unconscious knowledge which the native speakers of a language share, and which allows them to both speak and understand their language. While the primary focus of this guide is on Canadian English, many of the principles and theories discussed apply to all other languages as well.

REVIEW EXERCISE

Each of the statements below illustrates a concept found in Chapter One. For each statement, determine which concept is being illustrated. Do this by writing the number of the concept beside each statement. The first is done for you.

Concepts:

1. Linguistic Competence
2. Prescriptive Grammar
3. Descriptive Grammar
4. Universal (i.e., something common to all languages)

Statements:

4	All languages have a way of making negatives.
________	Speakers of Canadian English know that one way to make questions is to move an auxiliary verb ahead of the subject noun phrase.
________	Many nouns in English are formed by adding *-ness* to an adjective; for example: sadness, silliness, and happiness.
________	'brung' should never be used as the past tense of 'bring'.
________	Every language has a set of vowels and consonants.
________	Speakers of any language are capable of producing an unlimited number of novel sentences.
________	In English, there is no theoretical limit on the number of adjectives that can occur before a noun.
________	In the sentence "My friend is smarter than me", 'me' is incorrect because it is an object pronoun and this comparative construction requires the subject pronoun 'I'.

____________ In English, the plural is formed by adding either [-s], [-z] or [-əz] to the end of nouns.

____________ Every language has a way of forming questions.

____________ Speakers of Canadian English know that the different vowel sounds in the words ***bat, bet, but,*** and ***bit*** are crucial to their meanings.

REVIEW! REVIEW! Make sure you understand the terms listed below.

- creativity
- descriptive grammar
- generality
- grammar
- the human mind
- inaccessibility
- linguistic competence
- mutability
- native speaker
- parity
- prescriptive grammar
- speech organs
- speech perception
- universality

QUESTIONS? PROBLEMS? DIFFICULTIES?

CHAPTER 2. PHONETICS: THE SOUNDS OF LANGUAGE

Phonetics is the study of the articulation and perception of speech sounds. The important topics and concepts found in this section include

1. International Phonetic Alphabet
2. Segments
3. Sound Producing System
4. Consonant Articulation
5. Vowel Articulation
6. Phonetic Transcription
7. Suprasegmentals
8. Processes

PHONETIC TRANSCRIPTION

The speech sounds of language are transcribed using the symbols found in the International Phonetic Alphabet (IPA). Some things to keep in mind:

- Each IPA symbol represents one and only one speech sound.
- Each speech sound found in language corresponds to one and only one IPA symbol.
- Since symbols represent sounds, the same symbols can be used in whatever language that sound occurs. **See Tables 2.1** on **pg. 16** of the text for some examples of how the same symbol can be used in different languages.

⇒ The focus in this chapter is on learning the sounds of English and their corresponding IPA symbols. For examples of some sounds not found in English and their IPA symbols, see **Tables 2.28** and **2.29** on **pg. 51** of the text.

⇒ It is important to remember that IPA symbols represent sounds and not how that sound is spelled in a particular language. To indicate this difference, symbols are enclosed in [ ] brackets. Don't forget to use them!

SEGMENTS

Words typically consist of a number of segments (speech sounds). Doing phonetic transcription involves determining what these segments are, along with their corresponding phonetic symbols. In doing transcription, it can be useful, as a starting point, to determine the number of segments in a word. But, don't be fooled by spelling! Each of the following boxes illustrates a reason why we can't rely on spelling to determine the number of speech sounds in an English word.

Some words, letters or combinations of letters have more than one speech sound associated with them. In each of the example sets below, determine if the underlined letter (or letters) is pronounced the same way for all the words presented.

⇒	'o'	as in	hot	echo	woman
⇒	'c'	as in	careful	century	
⇒	'ou'	as in	should	tough	sound

Sometimes one speech sound can be represented using different letters or combinations of letters. In each of the example sets below, determine if the underlined letter(s) have the same or different speech sounds.

⇒	through	clue	shoe	too
⇒	real	see	sorry	Sheila
⇒	straw	talk	fought	lost

Many words in English contain double letters. Double letters do not necessarily mean that there are two speech sounds. Say each of the words below and determine if you pronounce the double letter twice.

street book mitten killer

Finally, many words in English contain silent letters. These are letters which we do not pronounce and which therefore do not correspond to a speech sound. Say each of the words below and determine if you pronounce all of the letters.

knife leave pneumonia catch

The above points also illustrate some of the reasons for using IPA rather than conventional spelling for doing phonetic transcription. In IPA, unlike in spelling, each symbol corresponds to only one sound and always the same sound! The lesson is . . . when you are doing phonetic transcription, you need to forget about spelling!

Practice! Practice! To get ready for transcription, try the following exercises.

1. Determine the number of speech sounds in each of the following words.

   a. thing ________________ d. phosphate ________________

   b. comb ________________ e. scene ________________

   c. psychic ________________ f. fright ________________

2. Say each of the following words. Which letters correspond to the first sound in each word?

   a. Thomas ________________ d. knee ________________

   b. unemployed ________________ e. choice ________________

   c. committee ________________ f. ease ________________

3. Say each of the following words. Which letters correspond to the last sound in each word?

   a. laugh ________________ d. lamb ________________

   b. sang ________________ e. use ________________

   c. bow ________________ f. choice ________________

SOUND PRODUCING SYSTEM

Human language contains a finite number of speech sounds, or phones. Segments represent these sounds. The system that produces these sounds includes the following.

⇒ **Lungs.** The lungs provide the moving air necessary for speech.

⇒ **Larynx.** The larynx contains the vocal folds (or cords) which provide the source of the sound. See **Figure 2.2** on **pg. 19** of the text for a representation of the larynx. The vocal folds can be positioned in different ways. The space between the vocal folds is called the glottis. The different positions of the vocal folds are called glottal states. There are four glottal states that you should be familiar with; see **Figure 2.3** on **pg. 20** of the text for a representation of each of these states.

- Voiced
- Voiceless
- Whisper
- Murmur

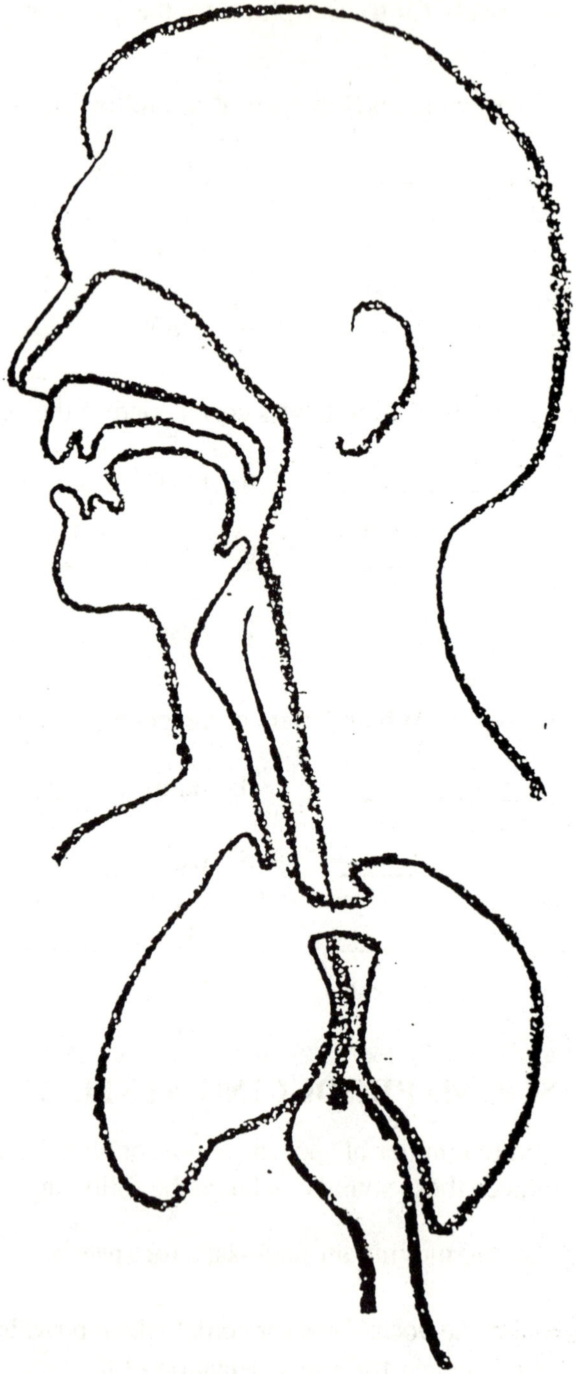

⇒ **Pharynx**. This is the tube of the throat between the larynx and the oral cavity.

⇒ **Oral Cavity**. This is the mouth.

⇒ **Nasal Cavity**. This is also known as the nasal passages. The velum controls airflow through the nasal passages. Raising the velum cuts off airflow through the nasal passages. Lowering the velum allows air to flow through the nasal passages.

The pharynx, oral cavity, and nasal cavity act as filters that modify the sound in various ways. Together they comprise the vocal tract.

Try this! Label the different elements of the sound producing system on the diagram on the opposite page. You can also label the trachea (windpipe) and the velum. If you're having difficulty, refer to **Figure 2.1** on **pg. 18** of the text.

SOUND CLASSES

Sounds can be divided into three major classes: consonants, vowels, and glides. Each class of sounds shares some phonetic properties. The defining characteristics of each class are given below.

⇒ **Consonants.** Consonants are sounds which can be either voiced or voiceless and which are made with a narrow or complete obstruction in the vocal tract. This is an articulatory characteristic of consonant sounds.

⇒ **Vowels.** Vowels are sounds which are typically voiced and which are made with little obstruction in the vocal tract. Vowels tend to be more sonorous than consonants. As a result, we perceive vowels as louder and longer lasting. This is an acoustic characteristic of vowels. Vowels are also classified as syllabic sounds, meaning that they can form the nucleus of a syllable.

⇒ **Glides.** Glides are sounds that have characteristics of both consonants and vowels. They are sometimes called semivowels or semiconsonants. Glides are like vowels in their articulation, but are like consonants in that they never form the nucleus of a syllable.

Exercise! Each of the following words has one or more letters underlined. The underlined letters correspond to one sound. Identify this sound as a consonant, vowel, or glide. The first is done for you!

1. rottweiler ___consonant___
2. through ________________
3. lovely ________________
4. year ________________
5. myth ________________
6. whistle ________________
7. suffer ________________
8. judge ________________

REMINDER!

Some types of consonants can also be syllabic (i.e., function as the nucleus of a syllable). For this reason, you should think of sounds not just as being consonants, vowels, or glides, but as being syllabic or non-syllabic elements. This will be useful in doing phonetic transcription and also when doing phonology (Chapter Three).

CONSONANT ARTICULATION

Consonants are sounds which are made with obstruction in the vocal tract. Consonants do not normally form the nucleus of a syllable and can be voiced or voiceless. The following pages contain information about consonants that you should become very familiar with.

Articulatory Description

All sounds, regardless of whether they are consonants, vowels, or glides, are described in terms of how they are articulated. This information is contained in the sound's articulatory description. Consonants and vowels are described differently. There are three parameters necessary to describe consonant (and glide) articulations.

1. Glottal State
2. Place of Articulation
3. Manner of Articulation

⇒ Glottal State refers to whether a sound is voiced or voiceless.

⇒ Place of Articulation refers to where in the vocal tract an obstruction occurs. Places of articulation are found

- At the lips (labial)
- Within the oral cavity (dental, alveolar, alveopalatal, palatal, velar, uvular)
- In the pharynx (pharyngeal)
- At the glottis (glottal)

Try This! Each place of articulation has an articulatory term used to describe sounds made at that particular spot in the vocal tract. For example, sounds made with the lips are called labial sounds. Give the articulatory term describing sounds made at each of the following places of articulation.

a. lips and teeth ______________________________

b. hard palate ______________________________

c. uvula ______________________________

d. alveolar ridge ______________________________

Now.... Label all places of articulation on the diagram on the following page. For each place of articulation, give the corresponding articulatory term. You can also label the different parts of the tongue (tip, blade, body, back, and root). If you are having difficulty, refer to **Figure 2.4** on **pg. 23** of the text.

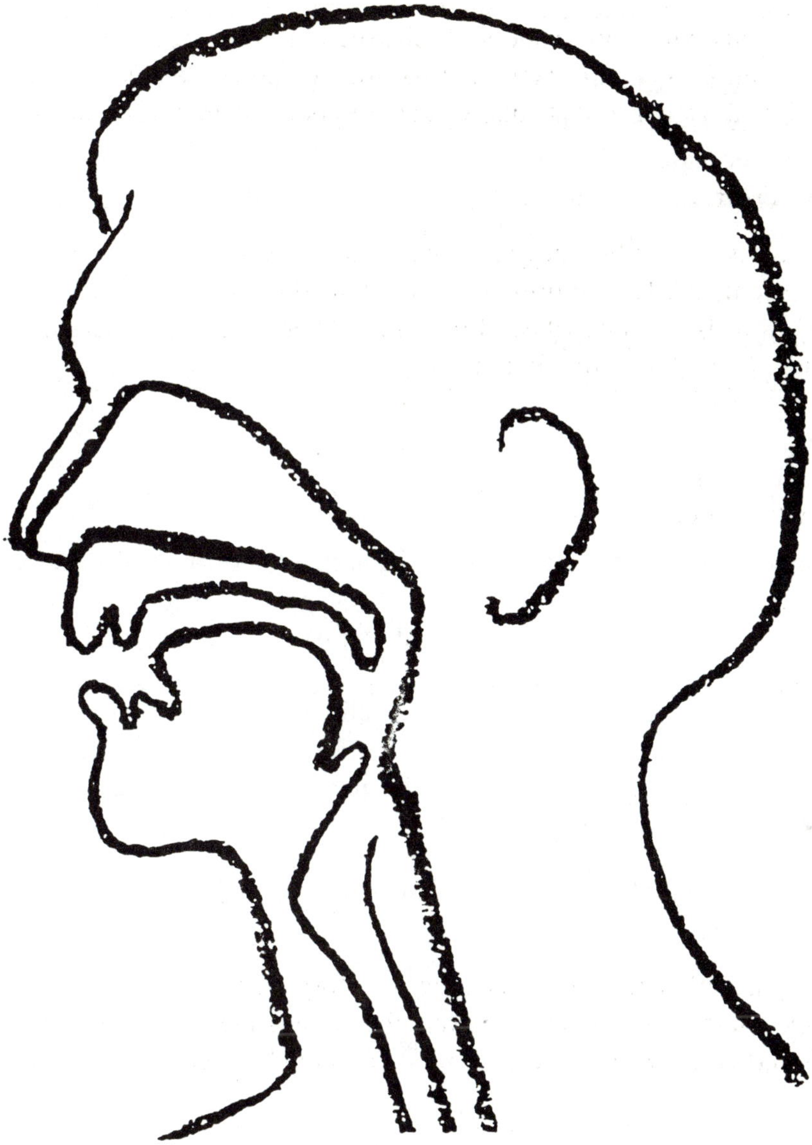

⇒ Manner of Articulation refers to the different types of sounds resulting from different positions of the lips, tongue, velum, and glottis. Manners of Articulation include

- Stops (see **Tables 2.3** and **2.4** on **pg. 26** of the text)
- Fricatives (see **Tables 2.5** and **2.6** on **pgs. 27** and **28** of the text)
- Affricates (see **Table 2.7** on **pg. 28** of the text)
- Nasals (see **Tables 2.3** and **2.4** on **pg. 26** of the text)
- Liquids (see **Table 2.10** on **pg. 32** of the text)
- Glides

Now.... Fill in the chart on the following page with the consonant and glide sounds of Canadian English. If you are having difficulty, refer to **Table 2.12** on **pg. 33** of the text.

Now try this!

1. Give the phonetic symbol for the first consonant in each of the following words.

   a. through ____________ d. whistle ____________

   b. shave ____________ e. phone ____________

   c. knee ____________ f. queen ____________

2. Give the phonetic symbol for the last consonant in each of the following words.

   a. laugh ____________ d. myth ____________

   b. sang ____________ e. lamb ____________

   c. choice ____________ f. box ____________

QUICK REMINDER!

Every sound has one and only one articulatory description. And every articulatory description corresponds to one and only one symbol in the International Phonetic Alphabet (IPA).

CANADIAN ENGLISH CONSONANT CHART

MANNER OF ARTICULATION	GLOTTAL STATE	PLACE OF ARTICULATION						
		Bilabial	Labiodental	Interdental	Alveolar	Alveopalatal	Velar	Glottal
Stop	voiceless							
	voiced							
Fricative	voiceless							
	voiced							
Affricate	voiceless							
	voiced							
Nasal	voiced							
Liquid a. lateral b. retroflex	 voiced voiced							
Glide	voiced							

Some more about....

Voiceless Stop Articulations

⇒ **Aspiration.** Sometimes when the voiceless stops [p, t, k] are pronounced, they are produced with a small puff of air. This puff of air is called aspiration and is represented as [ʰ]. Aspiration is caused by a delay in voicing.

Try This! Say the words in the boxes below. Pay close attention to the first sound, and see if you can feel when aspiration does and does not occur. You can feel this extra release of air by putting your hand close to your mouth as you produce the words.

Voiceless Aspirated Stops		**Voiceless Unaspirated Stops**	
[pʰ]	pit punk	[p]	spit spunk
[tʰ]	take tab	[t]	stake stab
[kʰ]	kill car	[k]	skill scar

See **Figures 2.5, 2.6**, and **2.7** on **pgs. 29** and **30** of the text for some diagrams outlining when and why aspiration does and does not occur in English.

⇒ **Unreleased Stops.** Sometimes when the voiceless stops [p, t, k] are pronounced they are not released. That is, the articulation ends with either the lips closed or the tongue on the place of articulation. The symbol for this articulation is a raised [˺].

Try This! Say the words in the boxes below. For the words in the first column, pay close attention to the first sound, and see if you can feel your lips opening or your tongue moving away from the place of articulation. For the words in the second column, pay close attention to the final sound and see if your lips remain closed or if your tongue remains at the place of articulation.

Voiceless Aspirated Stops		**Voiceless Unreleased Stops**	
[pʰ]	pit punk	[p˺]	cap leap
[tʰ]	take tab	[t˺]	pot most
[kʰ]	kill car	[k˺]	back sack

Fricative and Affricate Articulations

⇒ **Strident/Sibilant.** Some fricatives and affricates are noisier than are others. Say the words in the box below. See if you can hear which fricatives and affricates are noisier. The noisier fricatives and affricates are considered to be strident (sibilant). The quieter fricatives and affricates are considered non-strident. This is an acoustic criterion used in describing fricatives and affricates.

Non Strident Fricatives		Strident Fricatives & Affricates	
[f] and [v]	fit vat	[s] and [z]	sip zen
[θ] and [ð]	thick though	[ʃ] and [ʒ]	ship pleasure
		[ʧ] and [ʤ]	cherub gem

Now… Go back to the Canadian English consonant chart on pg. 17 and put a box around the group of fricatives and affricates considered to be strident. If you are having difficulty, see **Table 2.8** on **pg. 29** of the text.

Liquid and Nasal Articulations

⇒ **Clear and Dark l.** Not every lateral [l] is pronounced in the same way. Say the words in the table below. Pay close attention to where your tongue is when you articulate the [l] sound. See if you can feel if your tongue is more towards the front or back of your mouth. The [l] in the first group is considered to have an alveolar articulation, while the [l] in the second group is considered to be velarized. The alveolar [l] is often called the "clear l" and the velarized [l] the "dark l".

Clear l (alveolar)		Dark l (velarized)	
[l]	lip love lullaby	[ɫ]	swallow guilt silk

⇒ **Syllabic and Non-syllabic.** Liquid and nasal articulations can be either syllabic or non-syllabic. Remember that a syllabic sound (e.g. a vowel) forms the nucleus of a syllable. It is only when a liquid or nasal forms the nucleus of a syllable that it is considered to be syllabic. If the liquid or nasal does not form the nucleus of a syllable, it is considered to be non-syllabic. Say the words in the table below and see if you can hear when the liquid or nasal is syllabic, and when it is

	Some syllabic sounds	Some non-syllabic sounds
Liquids	twinkle father	lawn rain
Nasals	glutton winsome	engine master

non-syllabic. See **Table 2.11** on **pg. 32** of the text for some more examples of English syllabic and non-syllabic liquids and nasals.

Exercise!

1. Say the following words. Put a check-mark beside those words containing aspirated voiceless stops.

1. scratch ______________________ 4. pending ______________________

2. talk ______________________ 5. stripe ______________________

3. segments ______________________ 6. careful ______________________

2. Say the following words. Put a check-mark beside those words containing a syllabic liquid or nasal.

a. laugh ______________________ e. kitten ______________________

b. bottom ______________________ f. bushel ______________________

c. mad ______________________ g. rugby ______________________

d. suffer ______________________ h. note ______________________

3. Say the following words. Put a check-mark beside those words containing a velarized (dark) [ɫ].

a. malign ______________________ d. pull ______________________

b. silly ______________________ e. lamb ______________________

c. allow ______________________ f. meal ______________________

VOWEL ARTICULATION

Vowels are sounds which are sonorant, which are articulated with little obstruction in the vocal tract, and which are syllabic (can form the nucleus of a syllable). Vowels are also usually voiced.

Articulatory Description

Four parameters are necessary to describe vowel articulations.

1. Height
2. Backness
3. Tenseness
4. Rounding

⇒ Different vowel sounds are made by varying the position of the body of the tongue. High, mid, and low (height), and front and back (backness) are used to describe tongue placement.

⇒ Tenseness refers to the amount of constriction in the vocal tract muscles when the sound is articulated. Vowels made with greater constriction are described as tense. Vowels made with less constriction are described as lax. Tense vowels tend to be longer than lax vowels.

⇒ Rounding refers to whether the lips are rounded or not. Vowels with the lips rounded are described as rounded; vowels without lip rounding are described as unrounded.

Simple Vowels and Diphthongs

⇒ Simple vowels are vowels whose quality does not change during their articulation, while diphthongs are vowels that exhibit a change in quality within a single syllable. This change in quality is the result of the tongue moving away from a vowel articulation to a glide articulation. Say the words in the table below and see if you can hear the change in quality during a diphthong articulation.

Some simple vowels	Some diphthongs
sit	boy
lost	now
cup	cry
met	pray
bat	sew

⇒ Diphthongs can be classified as either major or minor. The major diphthongs are those whose quality change is easy to hear. The quality change in the minor diphthongs is harder to hear. Say the words containing diphthongs in the above table again and see if you can tell which are the major diphthongs and which the minor diphthongs.

See **Table 2.13** on **pg. 35** of the text for some examples of simple vowels, and major and minor diphthongs in Canadian English.

Some other vowels ....

⇒ [a] is found in Canadian English as a single vowel only before [r] in words such as *car*.

⇒ [ɔ] is found in Canadian English only before [r] in words such as *more*.

Now... Fill in the chart on the following page with the phonetic symbols corresponding to both the simple vowels and diphthongs found in Canadian English. Circle all tense vowels. See **Figure 2.10** on **pg. 37** of the text if you are having difficulty.

Practice! Give the phonetic symbol for the vowel sound in each of the following English words.

a. stool________________________

b. sight________________________

c. meet________________________

d. pot________________________

e. sit ________________________

f. put________________________

QUICK REMINDER

For every articulatory description, you need to be able to provide the corresponding phonetic symbol:

e.g., voiceless bilabial stop → [p]

For every phonetic symbol, you need to be able to provide the corresponding articulatory description:

e.g., [p] → voiceless bilabial stop

You need to be able to do this for both consonants and vowels!

CANADIAN ENGLISH VOWEL CHART

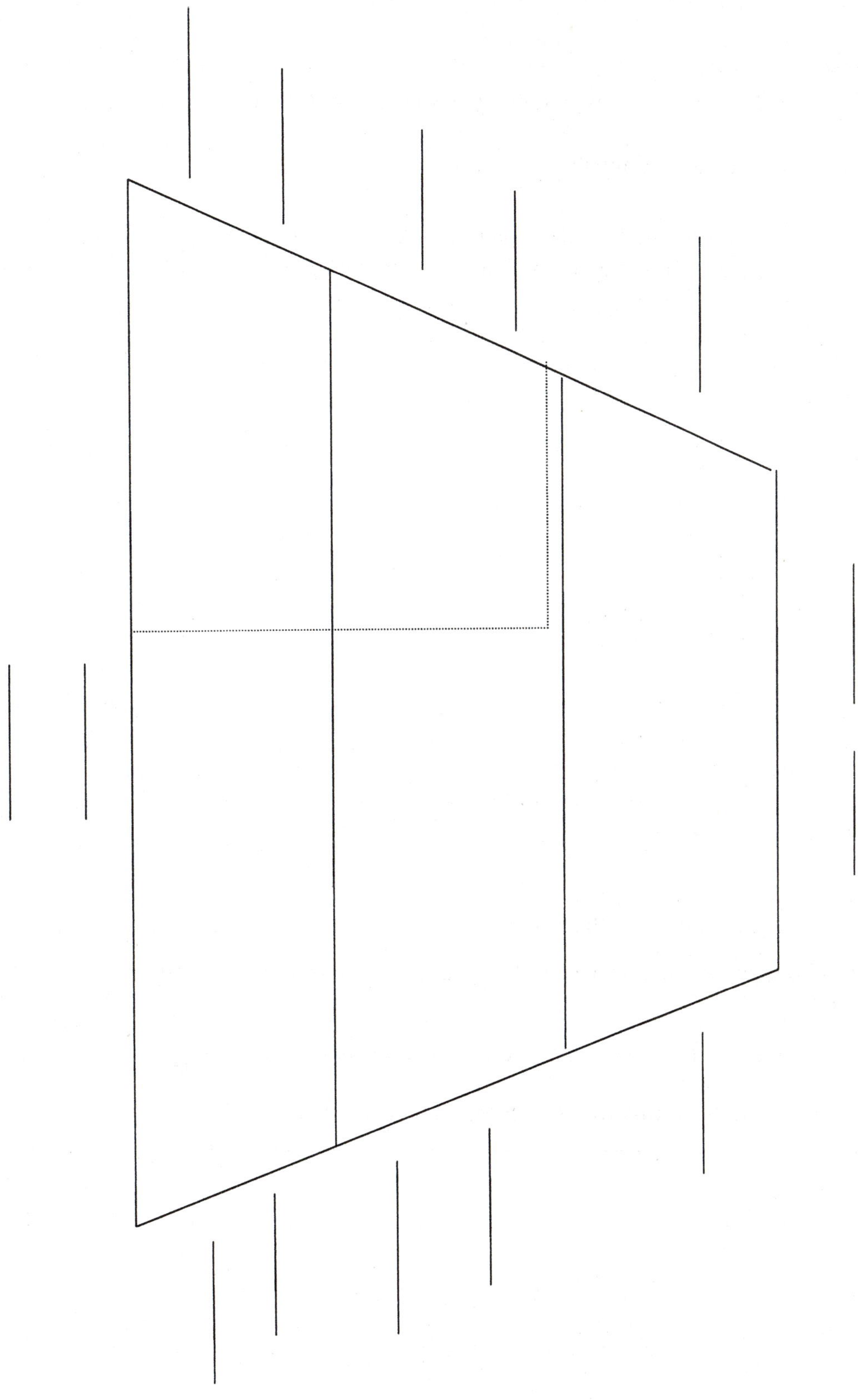

FACIAL DIAGRAMS FOR CONSONANTS

There are four important parts to either completing or deciphering facial diagrams for consonants.

Voicing / Voicelessness. Voicing is shown by two wavy lines where the larynx would be. Voiceless sounds are represented by two lines shaped like an ellipse.

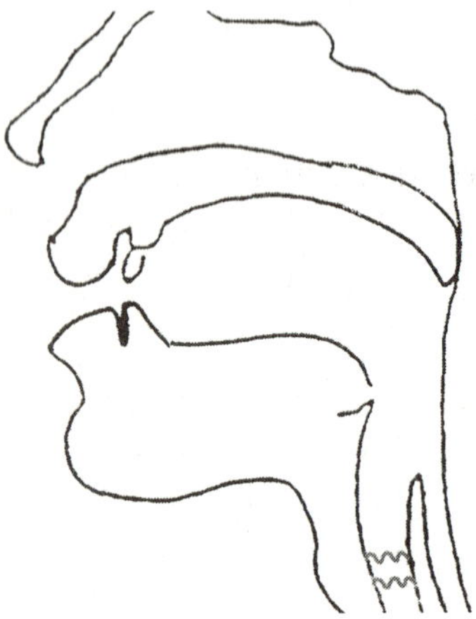

Voiced

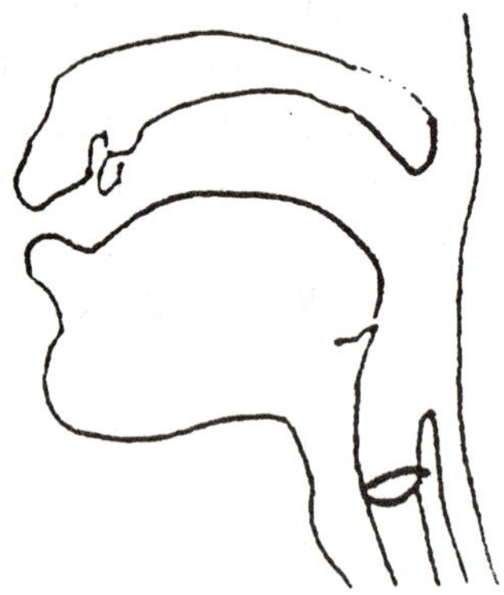

Voiceless

Place of Articulation. The narrowest point in the airstream passage is the place of articulation.

Manner of Articulation. If no air escapes past a given articulator (i.e., in a stop), then the articulator must touch the place of articulation. If the air does escape (i.e., in a fricative), then there is a space between the articulator and the place of articulation. If the sound is an affricate, then the diagram is shown with the articulator touching the place of articulation and an arrow indicating the direction in which the articulator moves.

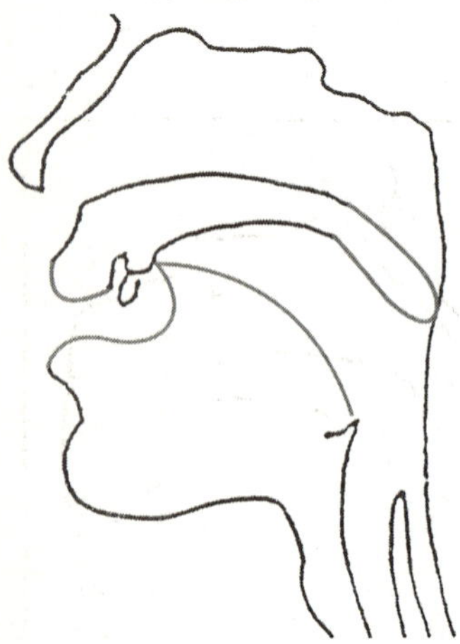

Stop

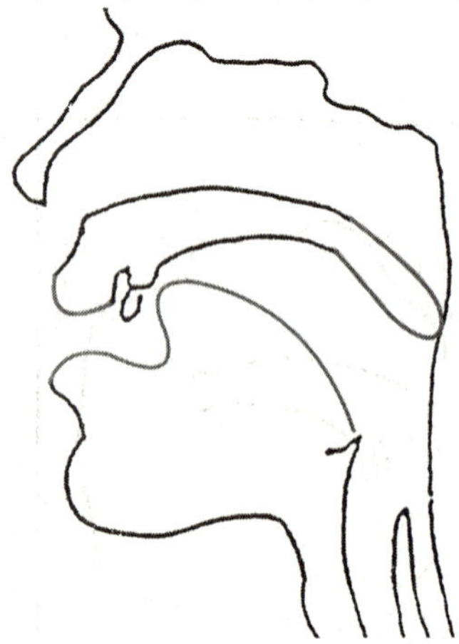

Fricative

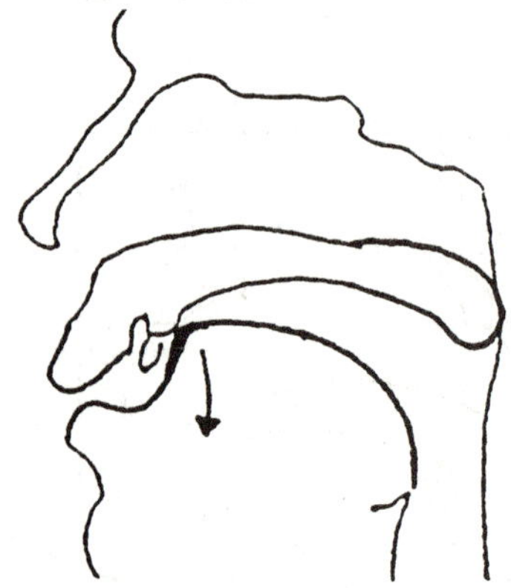

Affricate

Nasal Passage. For oral sounds, the nasal passage is closed, while for nasal sounds the nasal passage is open.

Complete the following diagrams so that each of the sounds listed below is depicted.

1. [s]
2. [p]
3. [ʧ]
4. [n]
5. [g]
6. [ð]

To complete the diagrams, you must:

- Draw in the glottal state: either voiced or voiceless.
- Draw in the lips: either closed or open.
- Draw the tongue to the place of articulation and to the manner of articulation.
- Draw in the velum: either raised or lowered.

The first sound has been done for you.

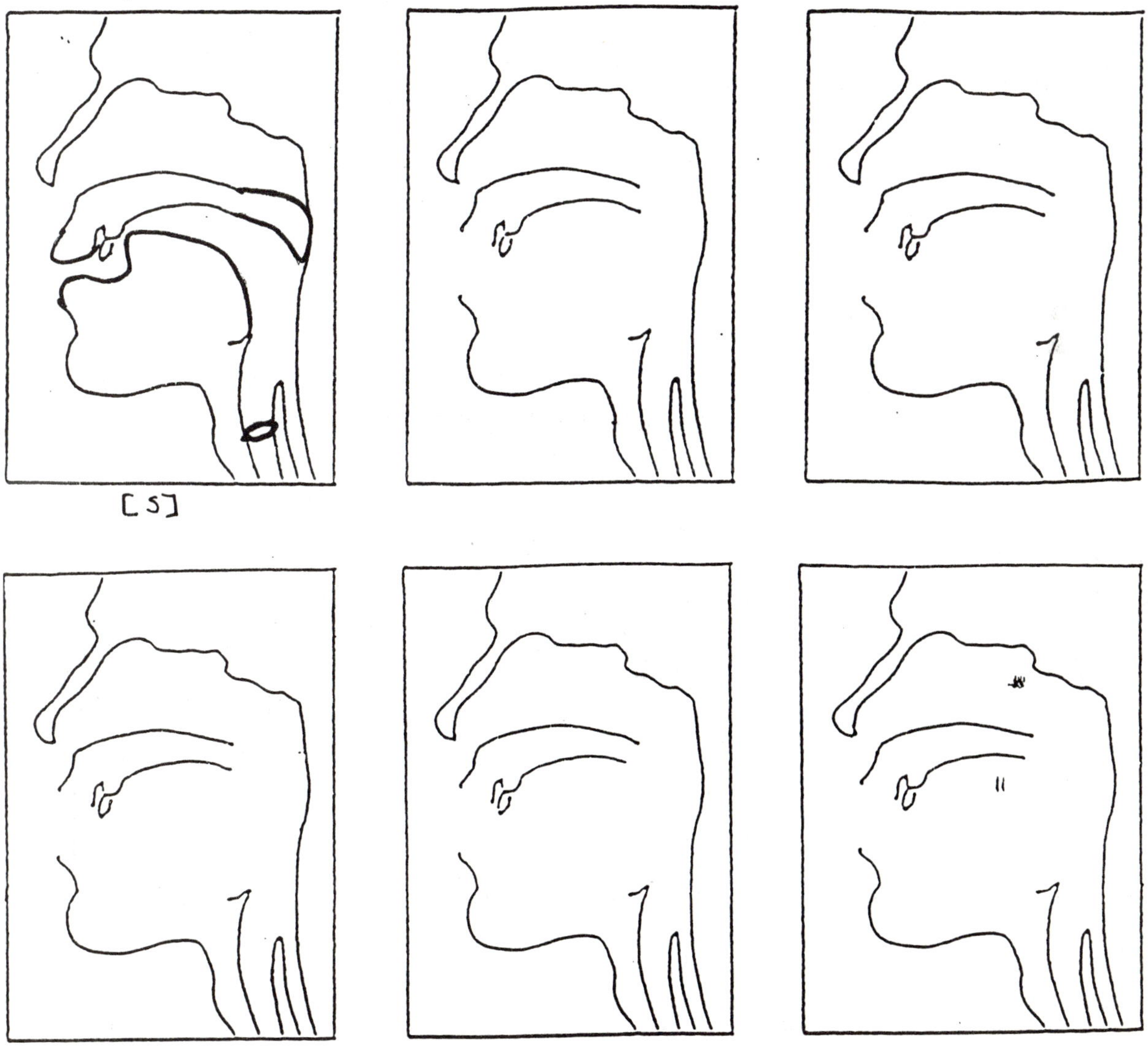

For each drawing presented below, there is only one sound that could be produced by the vocal tract position. You are to figure out which consonant sound is represented and write the phonetic symbol for that sound between square brackets below the drawing.

Make sure that you pay attention to voicing, place and manner of articulation and to the position of the velum.

The first drawing has been labelled for you.

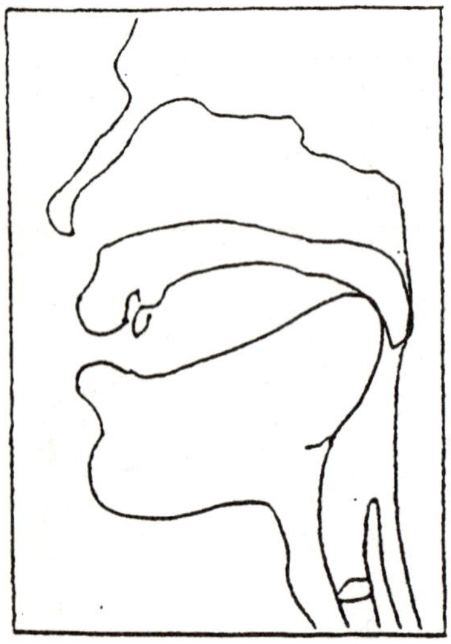

[K]

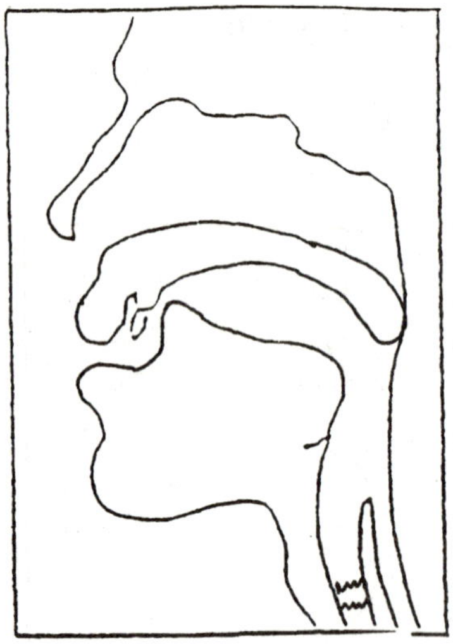

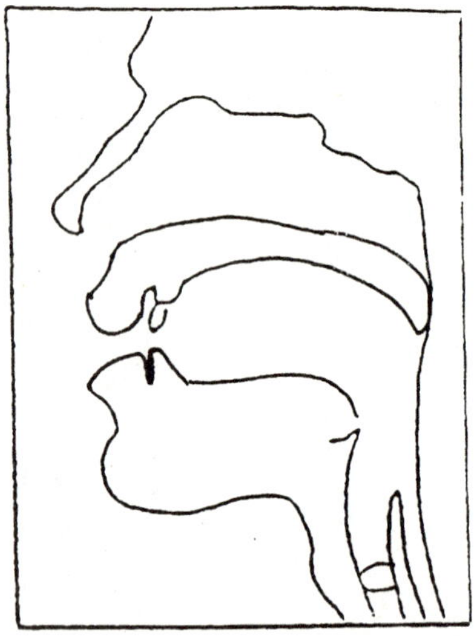

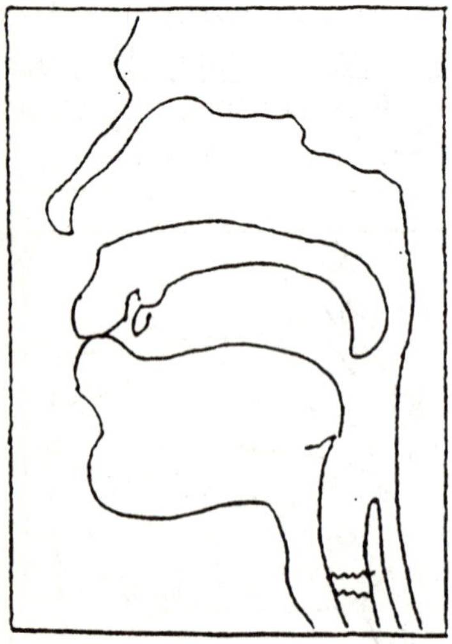

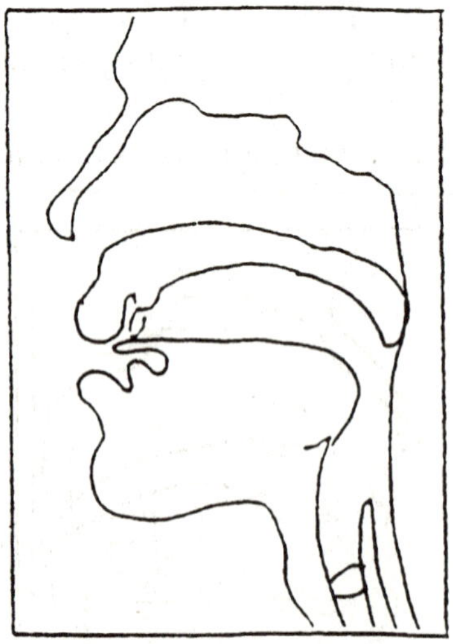

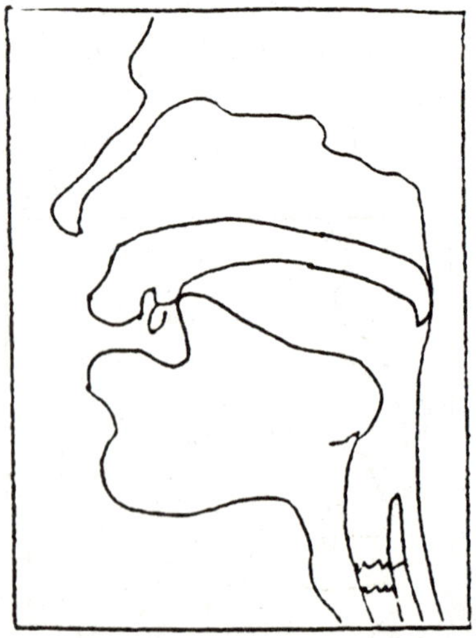

FACIAL DIAGRAMS FOR VOWELS

There are four important parts to either completing or deciphering facial diagrams for vowels.

Voicing. Vowels are always voiced. As on facial diagrams for consonants, voicing is shown by two wavy lines where the larynx would be.

Nasal Passage. For oral vowels, the nasal passage is closed, while for nasal vowels, the nasal passage is open.

Lip Position. Vowels are either rounded or unrounded. For rounded vowels, the lips are closer together, while for unrounded vowels, the lips are more spread apart.

Unrounded:

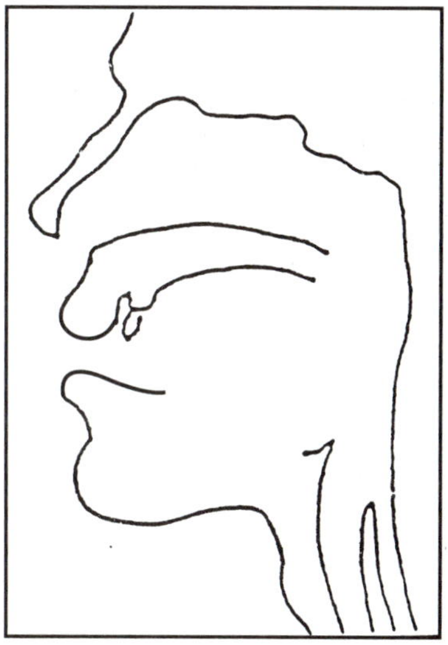

Rounded:

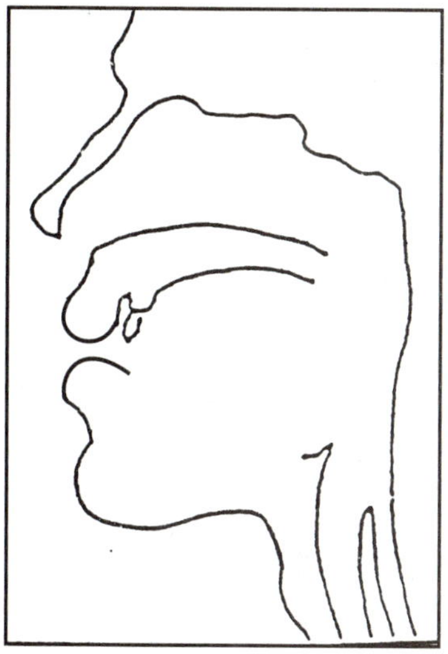

Tongue Placement. The height and position of the tongue determine the particular vowel articulation being depicted. For example, if the front of the tongue is high in the mouth, then a high front vowel results. Or, if the main body of the tongue is neither high nor low, then a mid central vowel results. Or, if the back of the tongue is low, then a low back vowel results.

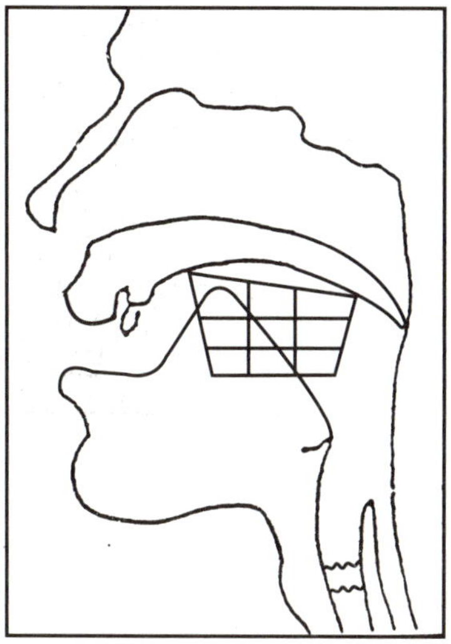

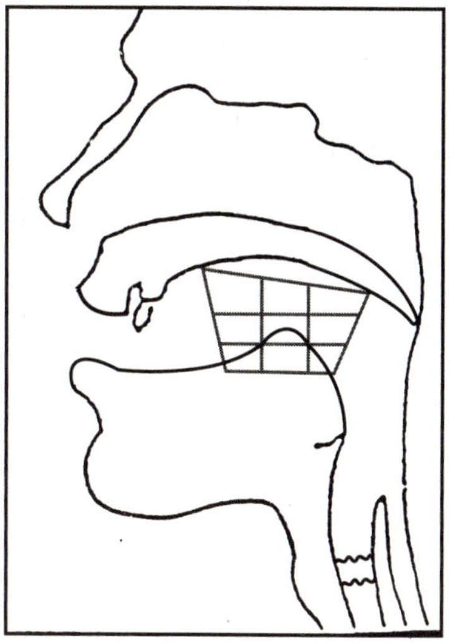

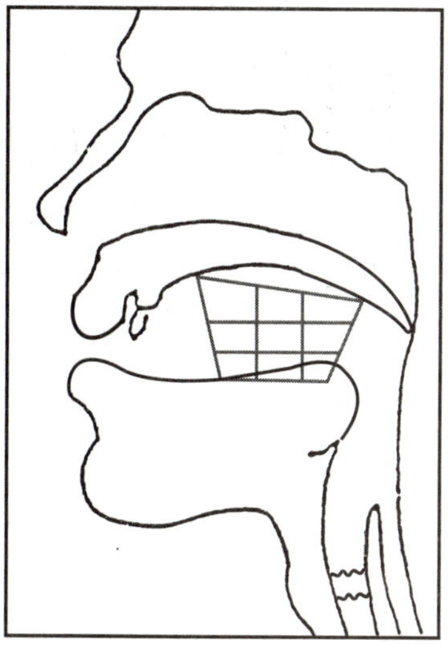

Complete the following diagrams so that each of the sounds listed below are depicted.

1. [æ] 2. [ʌ] 3. [ĩ]

To complete the diagrams, you must:

- Draw in the glottal state.
- Draw in the velum: either raised or lowered.
- Draw in the lips: either rounded or unrounded.
- Draw the appropriate portion of the tongue to the appropriate height.

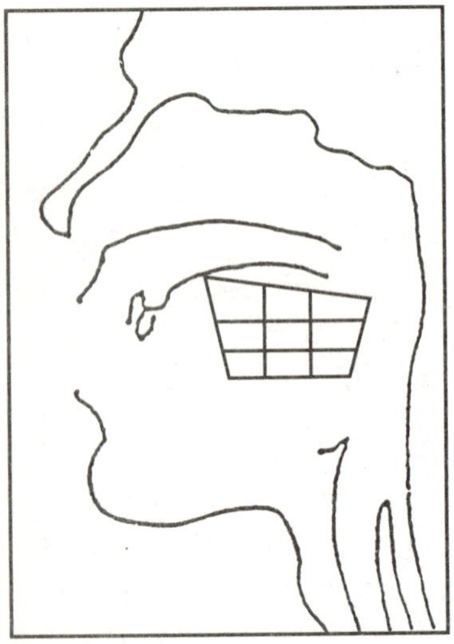

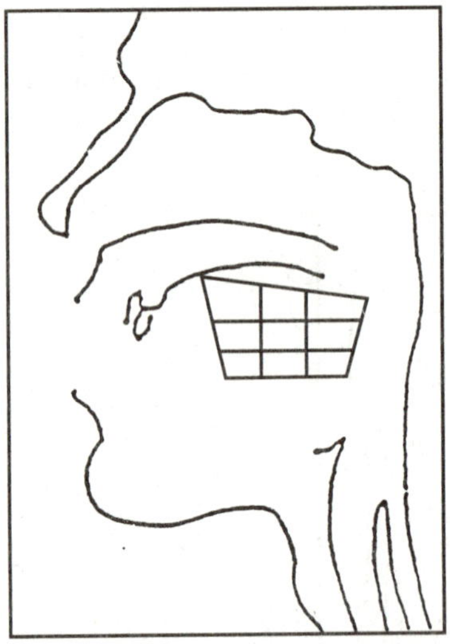

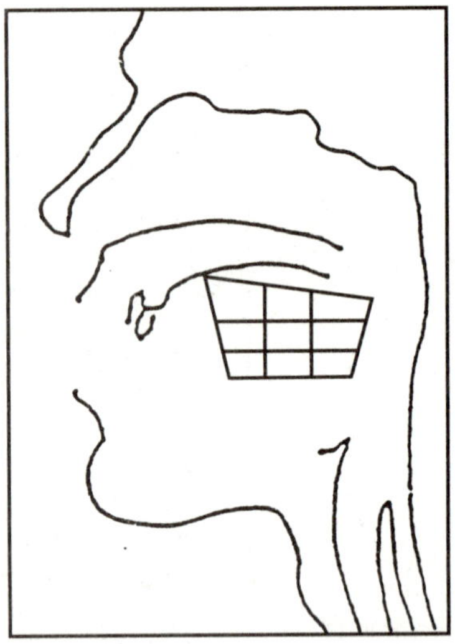

For each drawing presented below, determine which vowel sound is represented and write the phonetic symbol for that sound between the brackets below the drawing.

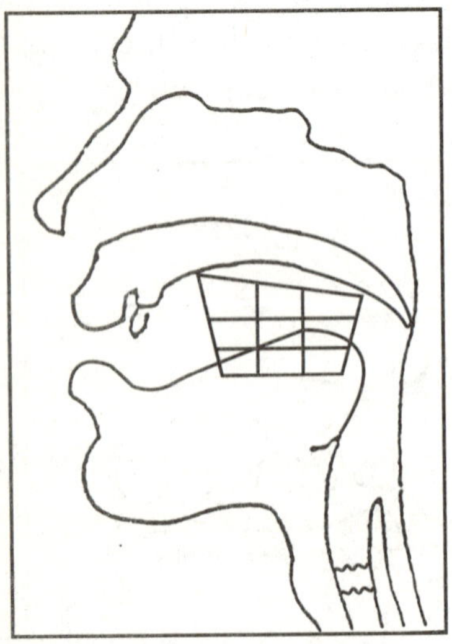

[ ] or [ ]

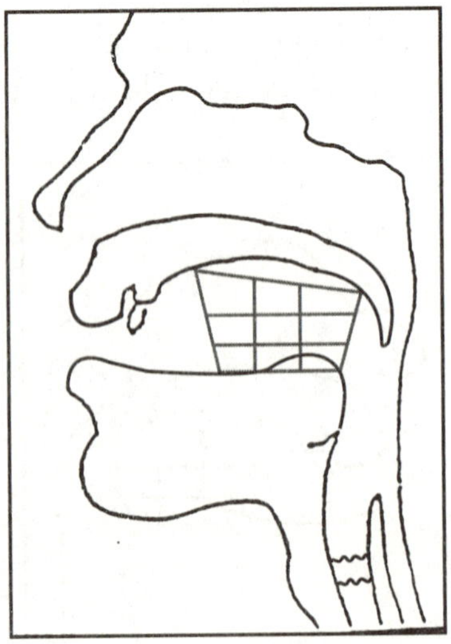

[ ]

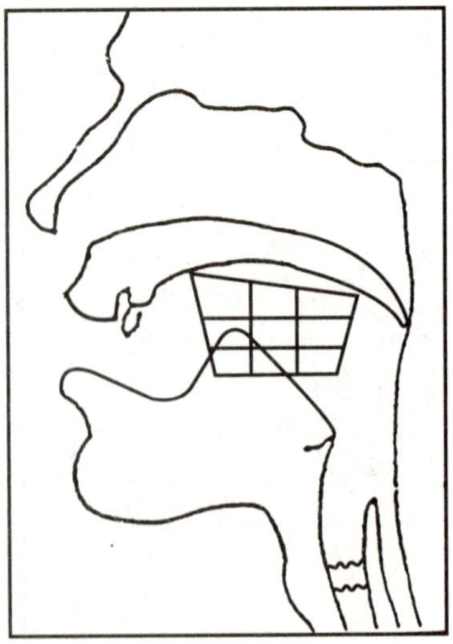

[ ]

PRACTICE WITH SOUNDS

1. Give the phonetic symbol for each of the following articulatory descriptions.

   a. [ ] voiceless glottal stop

   b. [ ] high front unrounded tense vowel

   c. [ ] voiced bilabial nasal

   d. [ ] voiceless interdental fricative

2. Give the articulatory description that corresponds to each of the following phonetic symbols.

   a. [æ] ______________________________

   b. [v] ______________________________

   c. [j] ______________________________

   d. [ʌ] ______________________________

3. Each of the following groups of sounds contains at least one shared phonetic property (e.g., glottal state, place of articulation, manner of articulation, tongue height, lip position, etc.). For each group of sounds, give some phonetic properties that the sounds have in common. Include as many as possible.

   a. [b, d, g] ______________________________

   b. [s, ʧ, ʒ] ______________________________

   c. [j, r, n] ______________________________

   d. [ɑ, o, ʊ] ______________________________

   e. [æ, ɪ, ɛ] ______________________________

4. For each of the following groups of sounds, circle the sound that does not belong and state a phonetic property which the remaining sounds share. There may be more than one possible answer!

   a. [f ð v m] ______________________________

   b. [d t n g] ______________________________

   c. [ɑ o ɪ u] ______________________________

TRANSCRIPTION HINTS

Each of the boxes below contains some examples of sounds that often cause difficulty when students are beginning to do transcription. For more examples of transcribed words containing Canadian English vowel and consonant symbols, see **Tables 2.16** and **2.17** on **pgs. 39** and **40** of the text.

SYLLABIC CONSONANTS

r	[r] for the 'r' sound in 'real', 'right', etc. [ər], [r̩], or [ɚ] for the syllabic 'r' sound in 'butter', 'bird', 'purr', etc. [ɾ] for the 't' sound in words like 'butter', 'writer', 'putter', 'potter', etc.
l	[l] for the 'l' sound in 'light', 'pill', 'please', etc. [əl] or [l̩] for the syllabic 'l' in 'bottle', 'puddle', 'poodle', etc.
m	[m̩] for the syllabic 'm' in 'bottom', 'winsome', etc. [m] for any other 'm' sound
n	[n̩] for the syllabic 'n' in 'button', 'hidden', etc. [n] for any other 'n' sound

DIPHTHONGS

Diphthongs are transcribed as vowel-glide sequences. Remember that diphthongs are a single speech sound. Remember as well that diphthongs are described in terms of the vowel, not the glide.

- Use [a], not [ɑ], for the major diphthongs (i.e., [aj], [aw], not [ɑj], [ɑw]). The symbols [a] and [ɑ] do not represent the same vowel sound.
- The mid tense vowels [e] and [o] are considered to be minor diphthongs and are transcribed as [ej] and [ow].
- The high tense vowels [i] and [u] are sometimes also considered to be minor diphthongs. You may be required to transcribe these as [ij] and [uw].

VOWELS BEFORE [r]

[r] is a very powerful sound, making it difficult to hear the preceding vowel sound. The following examples may help.

[bir]	beer	[bɔr]	boar	[bejr]	bear
[bar]	bar	[bur]	boor	[bər], [br̩], or [bɚ]	burr

SCHWA AND WEDGE

Schwa [ə]	Wedge [ʌ]
– used for unstressed vowels e.g., [əbawt] 'about' – found before [r] e.g., [bərd] 'bird' – used for the words 'the' and 'a'	– used when there is some degree of stress on the vowel e.g., [sʌ́pər] 'supper' – is not found before [r]

ASPIRATION

p,t,k	use [pʰ,tʰ,kʰ] for any 'p', 't', 'k' sound that occurs at the beginning of a syllable followed by a vowel that receives some degree of stress. e.g., [pʰæt] 'pat', [tʰɑt] 'taught', [kʰejk] 'cake' [əpʰír] 'appear', [ətʰǽk] 'attack'
	use [p, t, k] for any other 'p', 't', 'k' sound. e.g., [splæt] 'splat', [stɑp] 'stop', [skejt] 'skate'

You may also be required to transcribe

⇒ Unreleased voiceless stops. Use the symbol [˺].

⇒ Dark l. Use the symbol [ɫ].

[trænskrɪpʃən ɛksərsajzəz]

Transcribe the following words as you would say them in normal everyday speech. Remember to include brackets and remember to forget spelling!! Watch out for syllabic consonants!

1. craft
2. rich
3. thought
4. sigh
5. tape
6. had
7. health
8. vague
9. exit
10. azure
11. rooster
12. sugar
13. frog
14. instead
15. unit
16. paddle
17. bottom
18. question
19. angel
20. church

Vowel Practice!

1. key	2. cheese	3. bone
4. due	5. ate	6. east
7. loaf	8. wheeze	9. mainsheet
10. made	11. through	12. throw

More Vowels! This time watch out for vowels before 'r' sounds.

1. cheer	2. there	3. chair
4. car	5. star	6. score
7. sir	8. her	9. floor
10. oar	11. horse	12. course
13. heart	14. hard	15. harm
16. sharp	17. shirt	18. thwart

Practice with diphthongs. Transcribe the following words as you would in normal everyday speech. Watch out for those diphthongs!!

1. voice	2. trial	3. bicycle
4. hour	5. oily	6. price
7. eyes	8. prize	9. embroider
10. sight	11. sigh	12. sighed
13. prowl	14. counter	15. ice
16. knifed	17. down	18. daze

Remember … transcription takes a lot of practice!

Practice with schwa and wedge. In this one, pay close attention to the schwa and wedge sounds. You might want to determine which vowel gets primary stress to help you out.

1. sludge
2. thunder
3. hung
4. quality
5. behave
6. oven
7. luck
8. separate
9. stuff
10. nation
11. announce
12. understand

One more try! This one has everything in it!! Again, transcribe as you would in normal everyday speech. Watch out . . . they get harder!

1. days
2. agitate
3. gnome
4. Xerox
5. roast
6. sixths
7. guess
8. thumb
9. masculine
10. yellow
11. bargain
12. precious
13. science
14. machine
15. formula
16. motorcycle
17. surrounded
18. comedy
19. extinguish
20. costume
21. graduate
22. implement
23. writer
24. irrigate
25. isolate
26. timetable
27. unforgivable
28. frighten
29. lemonade
30. called

Reverse transcription. Give the correctly spelled English word for each of the following transcriptions.

1. [liʒər]
2. [ʃaj]
3. [pʰajp]
4. [æks]
5. [swit]
6. [sɑfənd]
7. [wərði]
8. [tʰub]
9. [fowni]
10. [wʌns]
11. [ʧojs]
12. [stæʧuw]
13. [ʃejd]
14. [mɛnʃən]
15. [skwɛr]

SUPRASEGMENTALS

Suprasegmentals refer to inherent properties that are part of all sounds regardless of their place or manner of articulation. The three main suprasegmentals are pitch, length, and stress. Pitch is further divided into tone and intonation.

Pitch

⇒ Tone Languages are languages in which pitch movement is used to signal differences in meaning. Mandarin Chinese is a good example. Tone languages may use register and/or contour tones. A register tone is a level pitch, while a contour tone is a moving pitch. See **Figure 2.13** on **pg. 42** of the text for some examples of register and contour tones in Mandarin. **Figures 2.11** and **2.14** on **pgs. 41** and **42** of the text give some examples from other tone languages.

⇒ Intonation is pitch movement that is not related to differences in word meaning. For example, rising pitch is often used to signal a question (an incomplete utterance), and falling intonation a statement (a complete utterance). See **Figures 2.15, 2.16, 2.17**, and **2.18** on **pg. 43** of the text for some examples of different intonations and their representation.

Length

⇒ Long vowels and consonants are sounds whose articulation simply takes longer relative to other vowels and consonants. Length is indicated with a [ː]. See **Table 2.19** on **pg. 44** of the text for some examples of short and long vowels in Yapese and **Table 2.20** on **pg. 45** for some examples of short and long consonants in Italian.

Stress

⇒ Stress is associated with vowels. Stressed vowels are perceived as more prominent than other vowels. The most prominent vowel receives primary stress. Primary stress is usually indicated with a [´]. In English, stressed vowels tend to be higher in pitch, louder and longer than unstressed vowels. See **Table 2.21** on **pg. 45** of the text for some examples of differing stress placement in English.

Exercise! Mark primary stress on each of the following words.

1. scorned
2. discovery
3. explosion
4. genius
5. macaroni
6. duplicate
7. dictate
8. occupied
9. informative
10. idolize

Now.... Go back and transcribe each word.

PROCESSES

Processes describe articulatory adjustments that occur during speech. Processes typically function to make words easier to articulate. Processes also occur to make speech easier to perceive. The boxes below define and illustrate the different articulatory processes found in language.

ASSIMILATION

Assimilation involves sounds changing to become more like nearby sounds. While there are many different kinds of assimilation, in general, assimilation can be divided into three main types:

1. Voicing Assimilation:
   - A sound takes on the same voice as a nearby sound
   - Includes: voicing
devoicing
2. Assimilation for Place of Articulation:
   - A sound takes on the same place of articulation as a nearby sound.
   - Includes: palatalization
homorganic nasal assimilation . . . and more!
3. Assimilation for Manner of Articulation:
   - A sound takes on the same manner of articulation as a nearby sound
   - Includes: nasalization
flapping . . . and more!

In addition ... some types of assimilation, such as nasalization, can be either regressive or progressive. In regressive assimilation, a segment takes on some characteristic of the following segment. That is, a sound is influenced by what comes after it. In progressive assimilation, a segment takes on some characteristic of the preceding segment. That is, a sound is influenced by what comes before it. See **Table 2.23** and **Table 2.24** on **pg. 48** of the text for examples of regressive and progressive place of articulation assimilation.

DISSIMILATION

A sound changes to become less like a nearby sound so that the resulting sequence of sounds is easier to pronounce, e.g., fifths: [fɪfθs] → [fɪfts].

DELETION

The process of deletion simply removes a sound from a phonetic context. Deletion frequently occurs in rapid speech, e.g., fifths: [fɪfθs] → [fɪfs]. See **Table 2.25** on **pg. 49** of the text for some examples of schwa deletion in English.

EPENTHESIS

The process of epenthesis adds a segment to a phonetic context. Epenthesis is common in casual speech, e.g., warmth: [warmθ] → [warmpθ]. See **Table 2.26** on **pg. 50** of the text for more examples of this process.

METATHESIS

Metathesis is a process that changes the order of segments. Metathesis is common in the speech of young children, e.g., prescribe → perscribe.

VOWEL REDUCTION

In vowel reduction, vowels move to a more central position when they are in unstressed syllables. That is, a vowel is pronounced as a full vowel when in a stressed syllable, and as a schwa when in an unstressed syllable.

Identifying processes ... To identify processes, you need to look for differences between the starting and ending pronunciations.

⇒ If a sound is missing, **deletion** has occurred.
⇒ If a sound has been added, **epenthesis** has occurred.
⇒ If the order of sounds has changed, **metathesis** has occurred.
⇒ If a sound has changed, you need to determine if either **assimilation** or **dissimilation** has occurred. To do this:

- determine the phonetic property that has changed (voice, place, or manner of articulation).
- compare this phonetic property with the phonetic properties of the nearby sounds.
- if the changed phonetic property matches a phonetic property of a nearby sound, then **assimilation** has occurred. The phonetic property that matches will tell you the specific type of assimilation that has occurred.
- if the phonetic properties do not match, then **dissimilation** has occurred.

Remember ... for assimilation, you also need to be able to identify when processes such as nasalization or place of articulation assimilation are regressive and when they are progressive. To determine this, you need to look at whether the influencing sound comes before (progressive) or after (regressive) the sound that is undergoing the change.

An example ...

prince: [prɪns] → [prɪ̃nts]

⇒ [t] occurs in the final pronunciation but not the starting; therefore, epenthesis has occurred.

⇒ [ɪ] has changed to [ɪ̃]. Remember that [˜] indicates a nasalized sound. The vowel, therefore, has changed from an oral to a nasal sound, and since the following sound is a nasal, assimilation, in particular nasalization, has occurred. The influencing sound is the following nasal, meaning that the nasalization is regressive.

The change in the pronunciation of the word 'prince' from [prɪns] to [prɪ̃nts] involves two processes: epenthesis and regressive nasalization.

Try these! Identify the process(es) at work in each of the following:

1. animal: [ænɪməl] → [æmɪnəl] ____________________
2. winter: [wɪntər] → [wɪ̃nər] ____________________
3. clear: [kl̥ir] → [kəlir] ____________________
4. puddle: [pʰʌdəl] → [pʰʌɾəl] ____________________
5. sixths: [sɪksθs] → [sɪksts] ____________________
6. wash: [wɑʃ] → [wɑrʃ] ____________________
7. sandwich: [sændwɪʧ] → [sæ̃mwɪʧ] ____________________

REVIEW! REVIEW! Make sure you know:

- the different parts of the sound producing system, including the vocal tract
- the difference between voiced and voiceless sounds
- the difference between nasal and oral sounds
- the characteristics of consonants, glides and vowels
- the places and manners of articulation for consonant sounds
- the different tongue placements required to describe vowels
- the difference between tense and lax, and rounded and unrounded vowels
- the symbols and articulatory descriptions for English consonants
- the strident fricatives and affricates
- the symbols and articulatory descriptions for English vowels
- when and why aspiration occurs
- how to complete and decipher facial diagrams
- how to identify processes
- the suprasegmentals of tone, intonation, length, and stress
- transcription, transcription, transcription!!

QUESTIONS? PROBLEMS? DIFFICULTIES?

CHAPTER 3. PHONOLOGY: THE FUNCTION AND PATTERNING OF SOUNDS

Phonology is the study of how sounds vary and pattern in language. The important terms, concepts and topics of discussion within this chapter include:

1. contrast
2. minimal pairs and near minimal pairs
3. variation
4. complementary distribution
5. phonemes and allophones
6. phonology problems
7. rules and generalizations
8. phonetic and phonemic transcription
9. syllables
10. features
11. derivations and rule-ordering

Since we will be dealing with many languages besides English, you will come across some phonetic symbols which have not been discussed. Articulatory descriptions will be provided for these unfamiliar sounds!

PHONOLOGICAL STRUCTURE

Three types of structure are relevant to the study of phonological knowledge.

Features: A feature is a unit that corresponds to a single piece of either articulatory or acoustic information. Features are the smallest type of phonological structure.

Segments: A segment is an individual speech sound. Each symbol in IPA represents a segment. Segments are comprised of features.

Syllables: A syllable consists of a syllabic element (e.g. a vowel) and any preceding or following segments. Syllables are comprised of segments.

These three units of phonological structure work together to produce the sound patterns of a language. See **Figure 3.1** on **pg. 57** of the text for a representation of the hierarchical relationship between the different units of phonological structure.

CONTRAST

Segments are said to contrast when their presence alone is responsible for forms having different meanings. Both consonant and vowel segments may contrast with each other. Determining which segments contrast is a first step in phonological analysis!

⇒ **Minimal Pairs.** A minimal pair is defined as two phonetic forms that differ by one segment that is in the same environment in both forms, and which have different meanings. Environment refers to the phonetic context in which the segment (sound) is found. A minimal pair means that sounds contrast.

e.g., English [pæt] 'pat' and [bæt] 'bat'

⇒ **Near Minimal Pairs.** A near minimal pair is defined as two phonetic forms that have segments in nearly identical environments. Like a minimal pair, these forms have different meanings, and like a minimal pair, a near minimal pair means that sounds contrast.

e.g., Hindi [bara] 'large' and [b̤ari] 'heavy'

⇒ **Phonemes.** Sounds that contrast are said to belong to separate phonemes. Part of native speakers' phonological knowledge includes knowledge of which sounds are contrastive (distinctive) in their language. Phonemes are used to capture this knowledge. Sounds belonging to separate phonemes can be represented as follows.

```
/ /          / /   ←——————   knowledge stored in the mind
 |            |
[ ]          [ ]   ←——————   sounds that come out of the mouth
```

Think... Which sounds contrast in the English and Hindi examples above? Put together a phonemic representation of the contrastive sounds in each example.

⇒ **Language Specific Contrasts.** Whether segments contrast or not is determined on a language-by-language basis. Sounds that are contrastive in one language may not be contrastive in another. Consider the following examples.

Language	**Segments**	**Phonetic Forms**
Khmer	[kʰ] [k]	[kʰat] 'to polish' and [kat] 'to cut'
Turkish	[ɛ] [æ]	[bɛn] 'I' and [bæn] 'I'
Japanese	[i] [iː]	[tori] 'bird' and [toriː] 'shrine gate'

Think... Do the sounds [kʰ] and [k] contrast in Khmer? What about in English? Do the sounds [ɛ] and [æ] contrast in Turkish? Think of an English minimal pair containing [ɛ] and [æ]. Do the sounds [i] and [iː] contrast in Japanese? Do they contrast in English? Remember that [ː] indicates a long sound.

See **Table 3.1** on **pg. 58** for some consonantal contrasts in English, and **Table 3.2** on **pg. 60** for examples of vowel contrasts in English. See **Table 3.4** on **pg. 61** of the text for some examples of vowel contrasts in Japanese and Finnish.

Exercise! State whether each of the following pairs of words is a minimal pair, a near minimal pair, or neither. Make sure you pay attention to the meanings provided.

1.	[bækt]	'towel'	and	[pækd]	'roof'	______
2.	[ʧogʊr]	'necklace'	and	[ʧogʊl]	'bracelet'	______
3.	[telʌm]	'book'	and	[tɛlʌm]	'book'	______
4.	[kətɑge]	'letter'	and	[kətage]	'fork'	______
5.	[supt]	'bulb'	and	[depts]	'sugar'	______
6.	[nozər]	'frog'	and	[hoʒəlʊp]	'valley'	______
7.	[fɪθæk]	'rain'	and	[fɪðæk]	'window'	______

VARIATION

Speech contains a great deal of systematic variation. Three types of phonological variation can be identified.

⇒ **Unpredictable Variation.** This refers to sounds which can occur in the same phonetic environment to create a possible word of the language. The variation is unpredictable because each sound can occur in the same phonetic context, and each occurrence creates a word with a different meaning.

- Unpredictable variation means that sounds are contrastive.

⇒ **Predictable Variation.** This refers to variation that is systematic. Predictable variation often affects segments which are phonetically similar. It is the result of the phonetic environment in which sounds are found, and which causes segments to be altered in some way. This variation is predictable, since it is possible to predict which sounds will and will not occur in a specific environment.

- Predictable variation means that sounds are non-contrastive.

⇒ **Free Variation.** This refers to sounds which occur in the same phonetic environment, but which do not create words having different meanings. Say the final *p* in the word *stop* in the following ways: (1) with the lips closed for a moment before releasing them ([stɑp˺]), (2) with a glottal closure ([stɑpˀ]), and (3) forcefully ([stɑp!]). Does the meaning of the word change with the different articulations?

Try This! Can the sounds [n] and [m] both occur in each of the following environments? What English words are created? What type of variation is this? Think about whether the words that result from using [n] and [m] in the same environment are or are not minimal pairs.

[_____ ajt] [_____ it] [pʰæ _____]

Can the sounds [i] and [ɛ] occur in each of the following environment? What English words result? Do these words have different meanings? What type of variation is this?

[l _____ʒər]

MORE ON PREDICTABLE VARIATION

The following exercises are designed to help you understand the nature of predictable variation.

1. In English, [p] has three phonetic variants:
   [p] – unaspirated
   [pʰ] – aspirated
   [p̚] – unreleased

   The following list of words gives examples of each phonetic variant.

[p]	[pʰ]	[p̚]
spook spirit operate hippy happening	pig police appear repair	collapse apt flipped ape cop clap

   On the chart below, put a check in the box if the phonetic variant can occur in that environment. The explanation of the different environments is given on pg. 44.

	#_____	_____#	s_____	_____C	V́_____V	V_____V́
[p]						
[pʰ]						
[p̚]						

Now… Can [p], [pʰ], and [p̚] all occur in each of the following environments? Think about whether the words that result from using each of these sounds in the same environment have different meanings. Then, determine which sound can occur in each of the following environments. Make sure you pay attention to which vowel is stressed.

[hɪ _____ i] [_____ ɑt] [kɛ _____ t]

2. English [l] has (at least) three phonetic variants:

[l] – alveolar (clear) l
[ɫ] – velarized (dark) l
[l̩] – syllabic l

The following list of words gives examples of each phonetic variant.

[l]	[ɫ]	[l̩]
lip	swallow	paddle
love	silly	obstacle
allow	salt	twinkle
malign	ilk	hassle
slip	pull	bushel
slide	meal	hurdle

On the chart below, put a check in the box if the phonetic variant can occur in that environment. An explanation of the environments is given on pg. 44.

	#____	C____V	V____#	C____#	____C	V́____V	V____V́
[l]							
[ɫ]							
[l̩]							

Now... Can [l], [ɫ], and [l̩] all occur in each of the following environments? Think about whether the words that result from using each of these sounds in the same environment have different meanings. Then, determine which sound can occur in each of the following environments. Again, be sure and pay attention to which vowel is stressed.

[s_____ ajd] [mi _____] [hæs _____]

Explanation of environments:

Question 1

# _____	word-initial position
_____ #	word-final position
s _____	after [s]
_____ C	before a consonant
V́ _____ V	between vowels (1st vowel is stressed)
V _____ V́	between vowels (2nd vowel is stressed)

Question 2

# _____	word-initial position
C _____ V	between a consonant and a vowel
V _____ #	word-final after a vowel
C _____ #	word-final after a consonant
_____ C	before a consonant
V́ _____ V	between vowels (1st vowel is stressed)
V _____ V́	between vowels (2nd vowel is stressed)

Reminder…. The above environments are not to be taken as a complete list of environments that can be used when doing phonological analysis. Many of the above environments (e.g., word-initial and word-final positions) are environments in which predictable variation is often found across languages. Other environments have been simplified (e.g., before a consonant and between a consonant and a vowel) and are applicable primarily to the exercises on the previous pages. They are not necessarily an accurate description of the environments in which the various sounds analyzed in these exercises are found.

Segments that are predictable may be in ……

COMPLEMENTARY DISTRIBUTION

Not all segments found in a language contrast with each other. Some segments are in complementary distribution. Two phonetically similar segments are in complementary distribution when they never occur in the same phonetic environment. Remember, the term "environment" refers to the phonetic context in which the segments occur.

⇒ **Distribution.** Sounds that are in complementary distribution are found in predictable environments. That is, they are an example of predictable variation. The distribution is simply a statement of the environments in which the sounds are found. In English, for example, oral and nasal vowels are in complementary distribution.

i.e., Nasal vowels occur before nasal consonants.
Oral vowels occur before oral consonants and after nasal consonants.

⇒ **Allophones.** Segments that are in complementary distribution are allophones belonging to the same phoneme. Allophones are phonetic variants of a sound. Part of native speaker knowledge includes knowledge of which allophones belong to the same phoneme. Remember that phonemes represent native speaker knowledge. Allophones belonging to the same phoneme can be represented as follows.

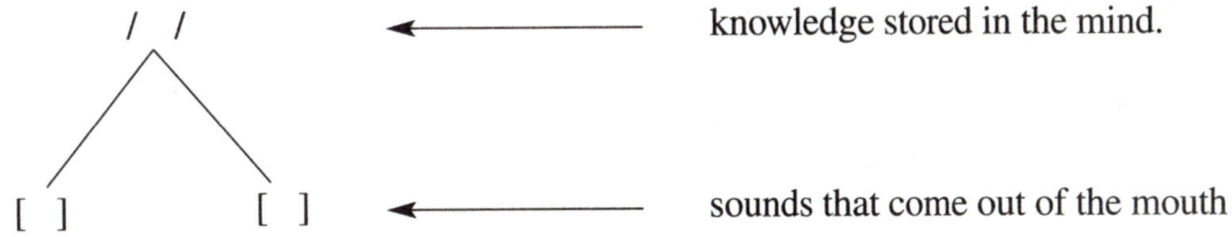

⇒ **Elsewhere.** One allophone is used to represent the phoneme. This is typically the allophone that occurs in the greatest number of phonetic environments and is referred to as elsewhere. So, the distribution of English nasal and oral vowels becomes

i.e., Nasal vowels occur before nasal consonants.
Oral vowels occur elsewhere.

⇒ **Language-Specific Distributions.** The patterning of allophones can vary from language to language. For example, both English and Scots Gaelic have nasal vowels; however, the distribution is different in each language. In English, nasal vowels only occur before nasal consonants. In Scots Gaelic, nasal vowels are found both before and after nasal consonants. See **Table 3.11** on **pg. 69** of the text for some examples of nasal and oral vowels in Scots Gaelic. See **Table 3.12** on **pg. 69** of the text for another example of variation in nasalization.

Think... How would the representation of oral and nasal vowels be different for Scots Gaelic than for English? Put together a representation of the English vowels [i] and [ĩ].

See **Table 3.5** and **3.6** on **pgs. 61** and **62** of the text for another example of complementary distribution in English.

THINK... of a language in which nasal and oral vowels are not in complementary distribution, but rather are contrastive!

DETERMINING COMPLEMENTARY DISTRIBUTION

For each data set below, find the complementary distribution and put together a representation of the distribution. Remember: the allophone that occurs in the greater number of environments is chosen as elsewhere and is used to represent the phoneme. All data is given in phonetic transcription.

1. The following data is from Oneida. Examine the sounds [s] and [z]. Note that [sh] represents [s] and [h] and not [ʃ].

[s]		[z]	
[lashet]	let him count	[kawenezuzeʔ]	long words
[laʔsluni]	white men	[khaiize]	I'm taking it along
[loteswatu]	he's been playing	[lazel]	let him drag it
[skahnehtat]	one pine tree	[tahazehteʔ]	he dropped it
[thiskate]	a different one	[tuzahatiteni]	they changed it
[sninuhe]	you buy	[wezake]	she saw you
[wahsnestakeʔ]	you ate corn		

2. Now examine the sounds [s] and [ʃ]. Again, [sh] represents [s] and [h], not [ʃ].

[s]		[ʃ]	
[lashet]	let him count	[ʃjatuheʔ]	you write
[laʔsluni]	white men	[tehʃjaʔk]	let you break
[loteswatu]	he's been playing	[jaʔteʃjatekhahʃjahteʔ]	they would suddenly separate again
[skahnehtat]	one pine tree		
[thiskate]	a different one		
[sninuhe]	you buy		
[wahsnestakeʔ]	you ate corn		

3. The following data from Japanese. Examine the sounds [t], [ʧ] and [ts].

The symbol [ts] is a single segment representing a voiceless alveolar affricate.

[tatami]	mat	[tsukue]	desk
[tegami]	letter	[ato]	later
[ʧiʧi]	father	[deguʃi]	exit
[ʃita]	under	[tsutsumu]	to wrap
[matsu]	to wait	[kata]	person
[natsu]	summer	[tatemono]	building
[ʧizu]	map	[te]	hand
[koto]	fact	[uʧi]	house
[tomodatʃi]	friend	[otoko]	male
[totemo]	very	[tetsudau]	to help

> ### QUICK REMINDER!!
>
> Don't forget to use / / brackets to indicate phonemes and to use [ ] brackets to indicate allophones.

PHONEMES AND ALLOPHONES

Phonemes and allophones are two units of representation used in phonology. These are used to capture native speakers' knowledge about how sounds pattern in their language.

PHONEME means ...
1. The way in which sounds are stored in the mind.
2. The contrastive phonological units of a language.
3. Underlying Representation.

ALLOPHONE means...
1. The way in which sounds are pronounced.
2. The predictable variants of the language's phonological units.
3. Surface Representation.

Contrastive sounds belong to separate phonemes and are represented on two levels.

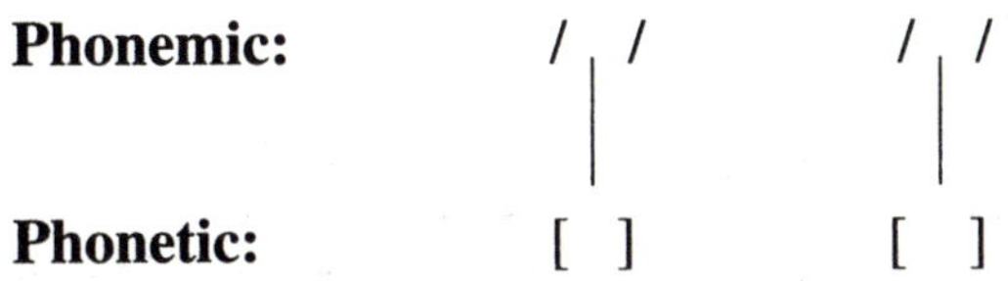

- Contrastive segments are phonetically different sounds (i.e., they have different articulations) *and* phonologically different sounds (i.e., they are found in unpredictable environments and make meaning differences).

Allophones belong to the same phoneme and are also represented on two levels.

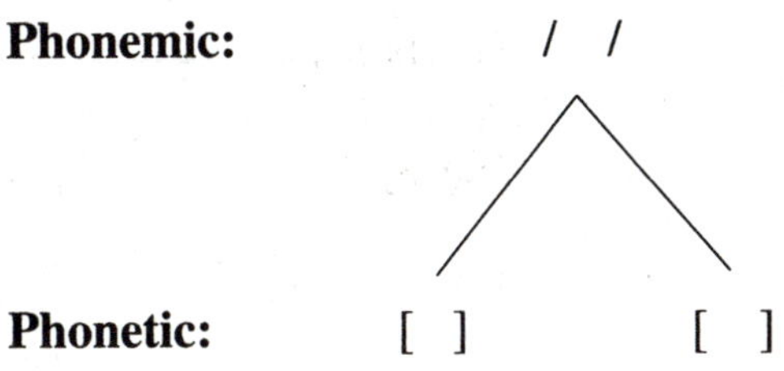

- Segments in complementary distribution are phonetically different sounds (i.e., they have different articulations), *but* phonologically the same sound (i.e., they do not contrast and are found in predictable environments).

SOLVING PHONOLOGY PROBLEMS

The basic goal in solving a phonology problem is to determine if the sounds being examined belong to the same phoneme or to separate phonemes.

WHEN ALLOPHONES BELONG TO SEPARATE PHONEMES, THEY ARE:

1. Contrastive/distinctive
2. In unpredictable distribution
3. Easily perceived as different
4. Not necessarily phonetically similar

WHEN ALLOPHONES BELONG TO THE SAME PHONEME, THEY ARE:

1. Non-contrastive/rule-governed
2. In predictable distribution
3. Not easily perceived as different
4. Always phonetically similar

PROBLEM SOLVING FLOWCHART

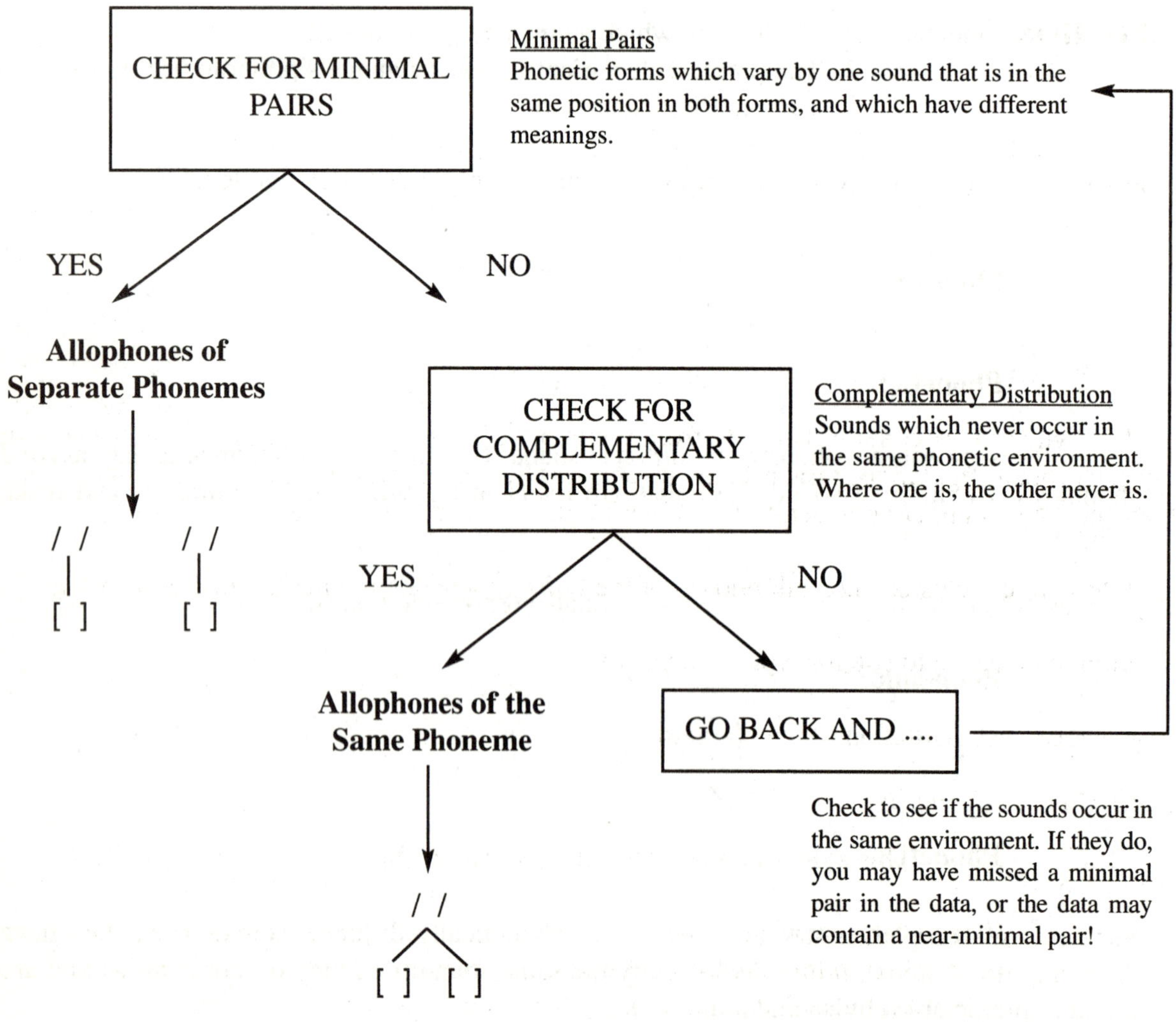

Repeat the above for each pair of sounds you are investigating!

1. Arabic: [h] and [ʔ]

a.	[ʔuruːb]	wars	e.	[huruːb]	flight
b.	[fahm]	understanding	f.	[faʔm]	coal
c.	[habba]	gust, squall	g.	[ʔabba]	grain, seed
d.	[haːl]	cardamom	h.	[ʔaːl]	condition

2. Hebrew: [θ] and [t] ([x] represents a voiceless velar fricative)

a.	[tafar]	saw	e.	[tannur]	stove
b.	[ʃtaim]	two	f.	[oθax]	you
c.	[iθi]	with me	g.	[teʃaʔ]	nine
d.	[raiθa]	you saw	h.	[tamid]	always

3. Slovak: [f] and [v]

a.	[vatra]	campfire	d.	[vɔlk]	wolf
b.	[farba]	paint	e.	[feltʃar]	paint
c.	[faːdni]	monotonous	f.	[vedro]	bucket

Think... Different languages may contain the same segments, but these segments may not pattern in the same way. Think about [t] and [θ] in English. Are these sounds in complementary distribution, or can they be found in a minimal pair? Put together a representation of how these sounds pattern in English. How is the English pattern different from how these sounds pattern in Hebrew?

SOME PHONOLOGY PROBLEMS!

The following pages contain data sets from a number of different languages. Some of the data may have been regularized. Each data set contains sufficient data to make valid conclusions about the sounds under consideration. For each data set, do the following:

- state your conclusion (i.e., allophones of the same or separate phonemes, or free variation)
- provide evidence to support your conclusion
- provide a representation of the phoneme(s)

1. Russian: [a] and [ɑ]

[a] This symbol represents a low central lax unrounded vowel.

Remember, you want to look for minimal pairs involving the sounds that you have been asked to investigate. There may be other minimal pairs in the data, but you only want those that contain the phones you are asked to examine.

1.	[atəm]	atom	6.	[pɑɫ]	he fell
2.	[dva]	two	7.	[dɑɫ]	he gave
3.	[pɑɫkə]	stick	8.	[dar]	gift
4.	[mas]	ointment	9.	[matə]	mint
5.	[ukrɑɫə]	she stole	10.	[brɑɫ]	he took

2. Inuktitut: [u] and [a]

[q] This symbol represents a voiceless uvular stop.

1.	[iglumut]	to a house	6.	[aniguvit]	if you leave
2.	[ukiaq]	late fall	7.	[ini]	place, spot
3.	[iglu]	(snow)house	8.	[ukiuq]	winter
4.	[aiviq]	walrus	9.	[ani]	female's brother
5.	[pinna]	that one up there	10.	[anigavit]	because you leave

3. English: [g], [gʲ] and [gʷ]

[gʲ] This symbol represents a 'fronted [g]' made with the back of the tongue at or near the hard palate.

[gʷ] This symbol represents a 'rounded [g]' made with simultaneous lip rounding.

1.	[gɑn]	gone	7.	[gʲik]	geek
2.	[gʷufi]	goofy	8.	[igər]	eager
3.	[gli]	glee	9.	[gejm]	game
4.	[slʌg]	slug	10.	[gowfər]	gopher
5.	[grin]	green	11.	[gædʒət]	gadget
6.	[rægʷu]	Ragu	12.	[gʲis]	geese

4. Korean: [l] and [ř]

[ř] This symbol represents a flapped [r].

[ʉ] This symbol represents a high central rounded vowel.

1.	[kal]	dog	11.	[silkwa]	fruit
2.	[kenel]	shade	12.	[mul]	water
3.	[iřumi]	name	13.	[seul]	Seoul
4.	[kiři]	road	14.	[kəřiřo]	to the street
5.	[juŋutʃʉm]	receipt	15.	[sařam]	person
6.	[pal]	leg	16.	[tatʉl]	all of them
7.	[ilkop]	seven	17.	[vəřʉm]	summer
8.	[ipalsa]	barber			
9.	[uři]	we			
10.	[onelppam]	tonight			

5. Tojolabal (spoken in Mexico): [k] and [k']

['] This diacritic means the sound has been glottalized.

1.	[kisim]	my beard	7.	[sak]	white
2.	[tʃak'a]	chop it down	8.	[k'isin]	warm
3.	[koktit]	our feet	9.	[skutʃu]	he is carrying it
4.	[k'ak]	flea	10.	[k'uutes]	to dress
5.	[p'akan]	hanging	11.	[snika]	he stirred it
6.	[k'aʔem]	sugar cane	12.	[ʔak']	read

6. English: [l] and [ɫ]

Note: The English data presented below has been simplified somewhat. For a more challenging (and more accurate) analysis of English [l] and [ɫ], try problem 10 on page 105 of the text!

[~] When this diacritic appears THROUGH a symbol, it means that the sound has been velarized. [ɫ] is a velarized lateral liquid. It is sometimes called the 'dark l'.

1.	[lɪp]	lip	7.	[fɪlθ]	filth
2.	[lʌvli]	lovely	8.	[wɑɫgrinz]	Wallgreens
3.	[sɪɫk]	silk	9.	[gɪlt]	guilt
4.	[slajm]	slime	10.	[gowfər]	gopher
5.	[mɪɫk]	milk	11.	[tæɫk]	talc
6.	[kæɫgri]	Calgary	12.	[hiəl]	heal

7. Sindhi: [p], [b], and [pʰ]

For these three sounds to be allophones of separate phonemes, you must find a minimal pair for:

- [p] and [b]
- [p] and [pʰ], and
- [b] and [pʰ]

You may use the same data item in more than one minimal pair.

1.	[pʌnu]	leaf	7.	[tʌru]	bottom
2.	[vʌʤu]	opportunity	8.	[kʰʌto]	sour
3.	[ʃʌki]	suspicious	9.	[bʌʤu]	run
4.	[gʌdo]	dull	10.	[bʌnu]	forest
5.	[dʌru]	door	11.	[bʌʧu]	be safe
6.	[pʰʌnu]	snakehood	12.	[ʤʌʤu]	judge

8. Kenyang (spoken in Cameroon): [k] and [q] Then: [b] and [β].

[q] This symbol represents a voiceless uvular stop.
[β] This symbol represents a voiced bilabial fricative.

1.	[enoq]	tree	7.	[uβit]	person's name
2.	[eβet]	house	8.	[nʧiβu]	I am buying
3.	[bag]	rope	9.	[etaq]	town
4.	[enok]	tree	10.	[nab]	brother-in-law
5.	[nbat]	knife	11.	[pobrin]	work project
6.	[etak]	town	12.	[ndeβi]	European

GENERALIZATIONS

Phonetic variation in language does not typically affect individual segments, but groups of sounds that share a common phonetic property: that is, classes of sounds. One of the goals of phonological analysis is to uncover and make generalizations about the broad patterning of sounds in language.

Some English examples ....

⇒ Liquids and glides have voiceless allophones after voiceless stops and voiced allophones elsewhere. See **Tables 3.7** and **3.8** on **pgs. 65** and **66** of the text for some examples.

⇒ The mid tense vowels are followed by a glide having the same backness and roundedness as the vowel.

Think.... What phonetic property do liquids and glides have in common that would make them pattern the same? What would be the phonemic representation of [ej] and [ow]? Remember that predictable information is not found in phonemic representations. How is this representation different from the representation of allophones belonging to the same phoneme?

Try This! In many dialects of Canadian English, [ʌj] and [ʌw] are allophones of /aj/ and /aw/ respectively. [ʌj] and [ʌw] are found before voiceless consonants and [aj] and [aw] are found elsewhere. This is called Canadian Raising. See **Table 3.9** on **pg. 66** of the text for some examples of words containing the allophones. Put together a generalization about these sounds. Think about the articulatory descriptions of the vowels. Remember that [a] is a low central unrounded vowel.

RULES

When a phonological analysis uncovers allophones belonging to the same phoneme, a rule can be put together to capture the distribution.

Some things to remember....

⇒ Allophones belonging to the same phoneme represent a predictable sound change. Such sound changes occur because segments are often affected by the phonetic characteristics of neighbouring sounds. These changes are described using processes such as assimilation. Rules, therefore, are descriptions of articulatory processes.

⇒ The sound changes represented in allophonic distributions usually affect classes of sounds rather than individual sounds. For this reason, rules are formulated as generally as possible.

The format and function of rules....

⇒ Rules are given in phonological notation.

e.g., $/l/ \rightarrow [\underset{\circ}{l}] \;/\; \left\{ \begin{matrix} p \\ t \\ k \end{matrix} \right\}$ ______

⇒ Rules link the phonemic and phonetic levels together.

1. The phoneme (e.g., / l /)
2. The change that takes place as captured by the non-elsewhere allophone (e.g., [l̥])
3. The environment in which the change from the phoneme to the non-elsewhere allophone takes place (e.g., $\left\{\begin{array}{c} p \\ t \\ k \end{array}\right\}$ ______)

- The rule is read as the statement 'A voiced lateral liquid becomes voiceless after voiceless stops'.

Think... What type of assimilation does the above rule describe? Think about the phonetic property of the phoneme that changed to arrive at the allophone.

See **Figures 3.18** and **3.19** on **pg. 97** of the text for examples of rules involving deletion and epenthesis.

Exercise! Convert these statements into rules. Watch out for classes of sounds!

1. Voiced oral stops become voiceless at the beginning of words.

____

2. Alveopalatal affricates become fricatives between vowels.

____

3. Vowels become nasalized before nasals.

____

4. Schwa is deleted word finally.

____

5. A schwa is inserted between a voiceless bilabial stop and a voiced lateral liquid.

____

Exercise! Convert the following rules into statements. Make your statements as general as possible.

1. $t \dashrightarrow t^{ʔ} \;/\; ʔ\_\_\_$

___

2. $\begin{Bmatrix} f \\ s \\ θ \\ ʃ \end{Bmatrix} \dashrightarrow \begin{Bmatrix} v \\ z \\ ð \\ ʒ \end{Bmatrix} \;/\; V\_\_\_V$

___

3. $\begin{Bmatrix} i \\ e \end{Bmatrix} \dashrightarrow \begin{Bmatrix} ɪ \\ ɛ \end{Bmatrix} \;/\; \_\_\_\#$

___

4. $\begin{Bmatrix} p \\ t \\ k \end{Bmatrix} \dashrightarrow \begin{Bmatrix} p^h \\ t^h \\ k^h \end{Bmatrix} \;/\; \#\_\_\_\acute{V}$

___

MORE PHONOLOGY PROBLEMS!

For each of the following data sets:

- determine whether the sounds under consideration are allophones of the same phoneme or separate phonemes, or whether they are in free variation. Provide evidence to support your conclusion along with a representation of the phoneme.

- If the sounds are allophones of the same phoneme, then provide a phonological rule.

While the data are from hypothetical languages, they exemplify phenomena found in real languages.

1. Storish: [ʃ] and [ʒ]

1. [gasaʃ]	mistake	5. [trutuʃ]	dive
2. [ʒipɑʃ]	head	6. [tolʒog]	crash
3. [sesor]	board	7. [naʒut]	hospital
4. [tʌʒəkəʃ]	ambulance	8. [ʧisoʃ]	operation

2. Nonamb: [i] and [ĩ]

1. [θikig]	weasel	5. [ɑpĩŋk]	fox
2. [gorĩm]	parrot	6. [nuret]	knife
3. [seyit]	arrow	7. [ʌlĩnd]	ferret
4. [kĩŋglɔn]	cave	8. [kuʧis]	deer

3. Skatik: [p] and [f]

1. [pʊnt]	scale	5. [lɔnik]	scone
2. [akog]	scatter	6. [jɪptu]	scold
3. [zifug]	skelter	7. [fʊnt]	skate
4. [jɪftu]	scare	8. [sipək]	skin

4. Severenese: [i] and [u]

1. [ubren]	table	5. [ublet]	never
2. [lezun]	clock	6. [seti]	blue
3. [gunob]	arm	7. [iplet]	stop
4. [setu]	moss	8. [ibren]	snow

5. Luru: [u] and [ʊ]

1. [luska]	stone	8. [surku]	to run
2. [holu]	fly	9. [umʊlo]	they have
3. [sʊrak]	left	10. [rukoru]	singing
4. [ketʊl]	arm	11. [uzmaluk]	road
5. [sumbu]	melon	12. [ketuʝ]	summer
6. [ambʊl]	yellow	13. [ʊrkʊl]	spark
7. [mastuf]	puppy	14. [mustʊf]	wine

6. Silliese: [t] and [d]

1. [madan]	joke	5. [tar]	chip
2. [tordalu]	club	6. [bondel]	laugh
3. [andar]	sneeze	7. [godu]	funny
4. [tili]	drink	8. [toko]	light

7. Breakie: [p] and [b]

1. [petikt]	juice	5. [lopibe]	milk
2. [dob]	sugar	6. [θupaz]	egg
3. [fæbe]	table	7. [bagur]	bread
4. [sepita]	food	8. [gitip]	salt

REMINDER! REMINDER!

When you find allophones of the same phoneme, there is a quick way to determine if your solution is in all likelihood correct. If your rule and statement describe an articulatory process such as assimilation, which is the result of neighbouring sounds interacting with each other, then your solution is probably correct. If your rule and statement do not describe such a process, then you might want to re-think your analysis!

PHONETIC AND PHONEMIC TRANSCRIPTION

There are two types of transcription: phonetic and phonemic.

⇒ **Phonetic Transcription.** Phonetic transcription is a representation of normal, everyday speech. That is, it is a representation of pronunciation. Phonetic transcription includes all phonetic information, both the predictable and the unpredictable. Phonetic transcription is always indicated with [ ] brackets.

⇒ **Phonemic Transcription.** Phonemic transcription is transcription that contains only the phonemes of the language. Phonemic transcription only includes unpredictable phonetic information: all predictable phonetic information is excluded. Phonemic transcription is always indicated with / / brackets.

⇒ **Understanding the Difference.** To help you understand the difference between phonetic and phonemic transcribe, go back to the Russian problem on page 49. Remember that in Russian [a] and [ɑ] are allophones of the same phoneme, with [ɑ] occurring before [ɫ], a velarized lateral liquid, and [a] elsewhere. Given this information, we can convert some of the Russian phonetic transcription into Russian phonemic transcription.

Phonetic		Phonemic	
[mas]	ointment	/mas/	ointment
[ukrɑɫə]	she stole	/ukraɫə/	she stole
[brɑɫ]	he took	/braɫ/	he took

- **Think...** does the phonemic transcription of Russian use the phoneme or the allophones? What about the phonetic transcription? Where is [ɑ] used in the phonetic transcription?

See **Table 3.15** on **pg. 71** of the text for some examples of phonetic and phonemic transcription of English.

⇒ **Inventories.** Since there are two levels of representation (phonetic and phonemic), a language will have two inventories of sounds. The phonetic inventory contains the allophones of the language, while the phonemic inventory contains the phonemes of the language. The phonetic inventory is used for phonetic transcription and the phonemic inventory for phonemic transcription.

See **Tables 3.17** and **3.18** on **pg. 72** of the text for partial phonetic and phonemic inventories in English.

Think... There are two levels of representation: phonetic and phonemic. There are also two types of transcription. What links phonetic and phonemic information together? Think about how you go from the phonemic level (knowledge) to the phonetic level (speech).

Practice! Practice! To practice phonemic transcription, go back over the phonology problems on pages 50–52, and wherever allophones of the same phoneme were found, convert the first few words in the data set from the phonetic transcription provided into a phonemic transcription. See if you can identify the predictable phonetic property that is missing from the phonemic transcription!

SYLLABLES

A syllable is a unit of representation consisting of one or more segments. There are five pieces of information crucial to understanding syllables, their structure, and their role in phonology. Make sure you know them!

⇒ **Syllables.** A syllable consists of a sonorant element and any associated less sonorous elements. Vowels usually form the core of the syllable, as they are the most sonorant type of sound. The core of a syllable is called the nucleus. Onsets are less sonorant segment(s) that occur before the nucleus, while codas are less sonorant segment(s) occurring after the nucleus.

⇒ **Syllable Structure.** Syllables have internal structure which is represented above the individual segments comprising the syllable. A syllable (σ) consists of an optional onset (O) and an obligatory rhyme (R). Rhymes consist of a nucleus (N) and an optional coda (Co).

⇒ **Universal Tendencies.** All languages have syllables. Tendencies in syllable structure across languages include:

- The nucleus of a syllable usually consists of one vowel.
- Syllables usually begin onsets.
- Syllables often end with codas.
- Onsets and codas usually consist of one consonant.

⇒ **Phonotactics.** Phonotactics is the set of constraints on which segments can occur together. For example, in English, [pl] is an acceptable onset, as in the word 'please', but [tl] is not an acceptable onset: words in English do not begin with this combination of sounds. Phonotactics can vary from language to language.

⇒ **Accidental and Systematic Gaps.** Not all combinations of sounds are found in the words of a language. Accidental gaps refer to non-occurring but possible forms, while systematic gaps refer to the exclusion of certain sequences. For example, the lack of words beginning with [ft] in English is not accidental but systematic, as such a sequence is unacceptable to speakers of the language. In contrast, that English does not have a word such as 'frip' is accidental, since many existing words begin with [fr] (e.g., frog).

Syllable Representations. There are three, sometimes four, steps to putting together a representation of a syllable. These are illustrated below for the word 'template'.

First: Assign the nucleus, the rhyme, and the syllable node. Vowels (including diphthongs) and syllabic consonants may occupy the nucleus position. (Diphthongs are often diagrammed as a branching nucleus.)

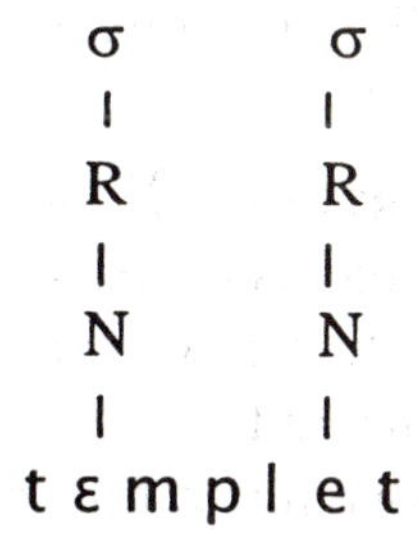

Second: Assign the onset. These are the segments to the left of the nucleus. Segments assigned to the onset are usually the largest sequence of sounds that can occur at the beginning of a word within a language.

Third: Assign the coda. These are the segments to the right of the nucleus which have not yet been syllabified into an onset.

Open syllables have no coda, while **closed syllables** have a coda.

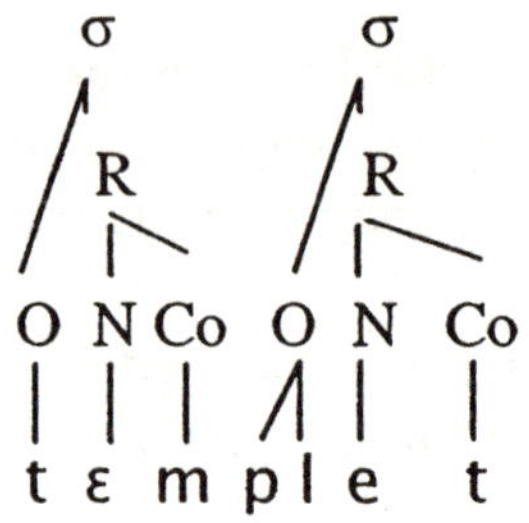

Fourth: As you can see from the representation being constructed, words can consist of a number of syllables. The last step in constructing syllabic representations simply involves combining syllables into words.

This step, however, is frequently omitted.

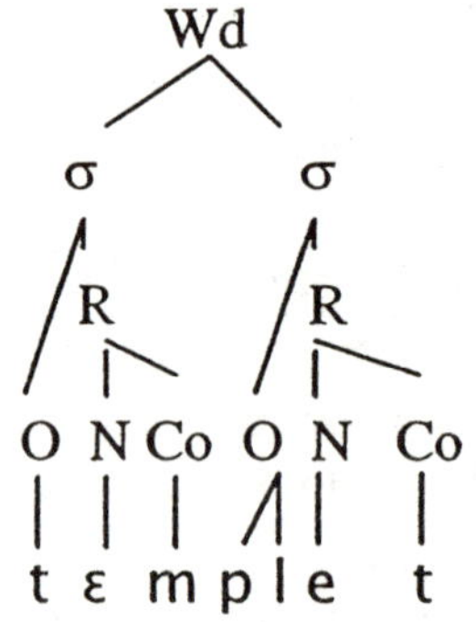

See **Figures 3.7, 3.8, 3.9,** and **3.10** on **pgs. 78** and **79** of the text for another example of the procedure for setting up syllables.

Try this! Construct a syllable representation for each of the following English words. Remember to transcribe the words first!

1. garden
2. downtown
3. banana
4. twinkle
5. understand
6. beauty
7. lovely
8. satisfy
9. property

Remember... To always assign onsets before codas.
This reflects a universal preference in language for onsets over codas.

Remember... That a syllable does not have to have either an onset or a coda.
A syllable, however, must have a nucleus and therefore also a rhyme.

Variation in Syllable Structure . . . Syllable structure can vary from language to language, yet the process for building syllable representations, as outlined above, can still be used.

Try This! In the hypothetical language data below, all syllables have the structure CV(C). This means that all syllables begin with an onset, but do not have to have a coda. That is, codas are optional. Construct syllable representations for following words. The data has already been transcribed for you.

1. [z i ʧ n o] 'chair'
2. [t a g k u] 'shell'
3. [s e d n a k u] 'sofa'

Syllables and Phonology . . . Syllables are often relevant to stating generalizations about the distribution of allophones. For example, in English,

- voiceless aspirated stops are found at the beginning of syllables and unaspirated stops are found elsewhere. See **Tables 3.22** and **3.23** on **pg. 80** of the text for some examples of English aspiration, as well as the distribution of aspirated stops in English.
- vowels are long when followed by a voiced obstruent in the coda position of the same syllable. See **Tables 3.24** and **3.25** on **pgs. 81** and **82** of the text for some examples of long and short vowels in English, including their distribution.

Try This! The data below is from the same hypothetical language as above. In this hypothetical language, stress is predictable, and is marked by a [´] over a vowel. Determine (making reference to syllable structure) where stress occurs.

Hint: You might want to first syllabify some of the words using the syllable structure constraints from above.

1. [fémba] foot
2. [hagút] month
3. [fezók] music
4. [waláp] mole
5. [supóspa] gravy
6. [tugábʧo] stone
7. [yumayumáp] armadillo
8. [póbzuʤi] lizard
9. [gaʧótfobi] knee
10. [talagubiták] cowboy
11. [páfzuliha] thin
12. [kéllaboga] arm

FEATURES

Features represent individual aspects of speech production. Features are usually divided into four categories, as shown below.

Major Class Features	Manner Features
⇒ [+/-consonantal] ⇒ [+/-syllabic] ⇒ [+/-sonorant]	⇒ [+/-continuant] ⇒ [+/-nasal] ⇒ [+/-lateral] ⇒ [+/-delayed release]
Laryngeal Features	**Place Features**
⇒ [+/-voice] ⇒ [+/-spread glottis (SG)] ⇒ [+/-constricted glottis (CG)]	⇒ [LABIAL] [+/-round] ⇒ [CORONAL] [+/-anterior], [+/-strident] ⇒ [DORSAL] [+/-high], [+/-low], [+/-back], [+/-tense], [+/-reduced]

Some important information ....

⇒ Since features represent articulation, they are always enclosed in phonetic (i.e., [ ]) brackets.

⇒ Features are binary and are specified either as plus (+) or minus (-).

⇒ [LABIAL], [CORONAL], and [DORSAL] are not specified as either plus or minus, but rather are used to represent the articulator that is active in executing the articulation.

- [LABIAL] for the lips;
- [CORONAL] for the tongue tip or blade; and
- [DORSAL] for the body of the tongue.

⇒ Place features are used to represent place of articulation features specific to the active articulator. That is, [LABIAL] sounds are [+/-round]; [CORONAL] sounds are [+/-anterior] and [+/-strident]; and [DORSAL] sounds are [+/-high], [+/-low], [+/-back], [+/-tense] and [+/-reduced]. See **Table 3.30** on **pg. 90** of the text for the representation of place of articulation features in some English consonants, and **Table 3.31** on **pg. 91** of the text for the representation of place of articulation in some English vowels.

Features are used ....

⇒ To represent segments. Each segment consists of a number of features, each of which represents either some articulatory or some acoustic information about articulation. See **Figure 3.12** on **pg. 83** of the text for an example of how features represent segments. See **Tables 3.32** and **3.33** on **pgs. 92** and **93** of the text for the feature matrices of English consonants and vowels.

⇒ To capture natural classes. Natural classes are classes of sounds that share a feature or features and that pattern together in sound systems. For example, voiceless stops can be considered a natural class, as can rounded vowels. See **Table 3.26** on **pg. 84** for an example of how features capture different natural classes.

⇒ To understand the nature of allophonic variation. Allophonic variation is not the substitution of one allophone for another, but a change in the specification of a feature of the allophone. For example, voiceless sounds often change and become voiced when near other voiced sounds. This can be captured with the single feature [voice].

<u>Determining feature representations ...</u>

⇒ **For segments.** Think about the articulatory description for that sound. Begin with the major class features and include in the matrix the appropriate value for each feature, so that when the features are taken together they define whether the segment is a consonant (obstruent or sonorant), a glide, or a vowel. Do the same for the manner, laryngeal, and place features. Remember for the place features, you need to first determine the active articulator, and then the features corresponding to the exact position of that articulator.

[p] is a voiceless bilabial unaspirated stop	Features	
	+ consonantal - syllabic - sonorant	these features define [p] as an obstruent
	- continuant - delayed release	these features define [p] as a stop
	- voice - SG	these features define [p] as voiceless and unaspirated
	o LABIAL - round	these features specify LABIAL as the active articulator for [p] and that the lips are not rounded.

⇒ **For natural classes.** Remember that a natural class shares a feature or group of features. Think about the features that the natural class shares. Include in the matrix only those features that all members of the natural class share.

voiceless unaspirated stops (i.e., [p, t, k])

$$\begin{pmatrix} +\text{consonantal} \\ -\text{syllabic} \\ -\text{sonorant} \\ -\text{continuant} \\ -\text{delayed release} \\ -\text{voice} \\ -\text{SG} \end{pmatrix}$$

- + consonantal, - syllabic, - sonorant: these features define all members as obstruents
- - continuant, - delayed release: these features define all members as stops
- - voice, - SG: these features define all members as voiceless and unaspirated

Note that place features have not been included in the matrix. This is because [p,t,k] each have a different place of articulation.

⇒ **For allophonic variation.** Remember that allophones are the predictable variants of phonemes and that their distribution can be described using a rule. Remember as well that rules have three parts: an individual phoneme or class of contrastive sounds, the allophone or change, and the environment in which the change occurs. Include features for each component of the rule. For the allophone, or change, only include the feature that changed from the contrastive sound(s). Some environments such as word- or syllable-initial, or word- or syllable-final, do not need features!

- For example, the rule (given here as a statement) 'voiceless unaspirated stops become aspirated syllable initially' can be formulated using feature notation as shown below.

$$\begin{pmatrix} +\text{consonantal} \\ -\text{syllabic} \\ -\text{sonorant} \\ -\text{continuant} \\ -\text{delayed release} \\ -\text{voice} \\ -\text{SG} \end{pmatrix} \longrightarrow [+\text{SG}] \;/\; \sigma \underline{\qquad\qquad}$$

See **Figure 3.21** on **pg. 98** of the text for another example of a rule referring to syllable structure.

Try This! Go back over the rules and/or statements you constructed for the exercises on rules and formulate them using feature matrices rather than phonetic symbols.

FEATURE EXERCISES

1. State the feature that distinguishes each of the following pairs of sounds. (There may be more than one correct answer.) The first is done for you.

   a. [θ] / [ð] ____[+/– voice]____

   b. [p] / [f] ____________________

   c. [s] / [θ] ____________________

   d. [b] / [m] ____________________

   e. [ʧ] / [ʃ] ____________________

2. Each of the following sets contains three sounds which belong to the same natural class. Add one other segment to each set, making sure that the natural class is preserved. Indicate the feature (including its value) which distinguishes the natural class. The first is done for you.

	Segment Added	Distinguishing Feature
a. [l̩ ə n̩]	[o]	[+ syllabic]
b. [θ s f]	[ ]	______
c. [p m k]	[ ]	______
d. [j r n]	[ ]	______
e. [ð f s]	[ ]	______

3. Name the natural class which each of the following phonetic matrices describe.

   a. [- consonantal, - syllabic]

   b. [+consonantal, -syllabic, -sonorant, +continuant, +voice]

4. In each of the sets below, all the sounds except one constitute a natural class. Draw a circle around the sound which does not belong and state the feature which the remaining sounds share.

   a. [t g v ʤ] ______________________________

   b. [j m ʒ w] ______________________________

   c. [m g d r] ______________________________

   d. [ʧ m t ŋ] ______________________________

5. In each consonant system below, some segments are boxed. Determine if the boxed segments constitute a natural class. If they do, then state the feature(s) that make them a natural class.

a.
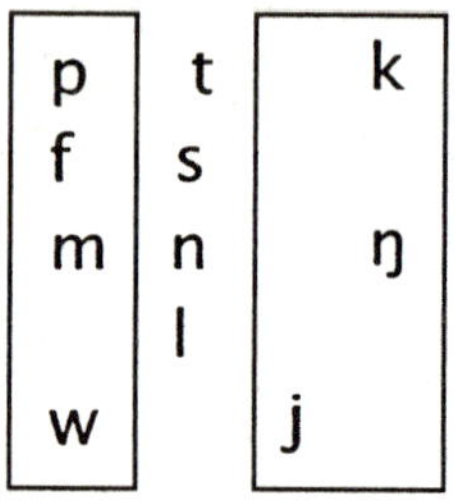

b.
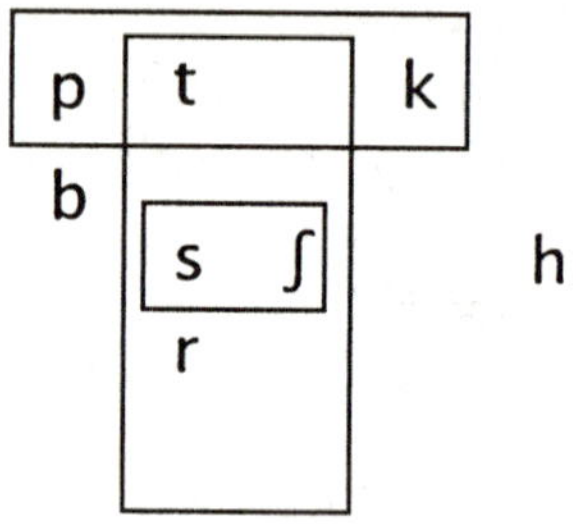

c.
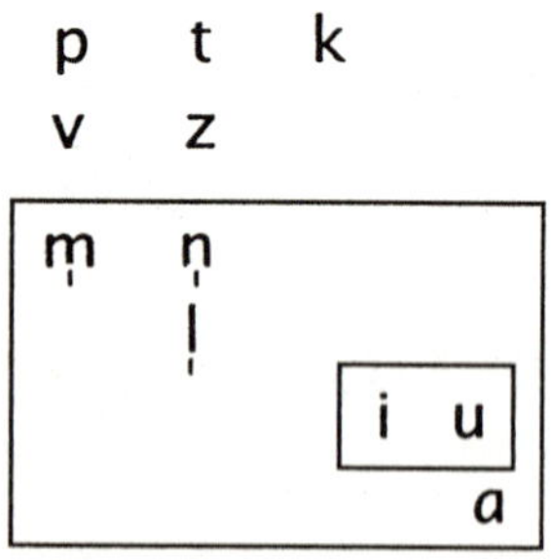

d.
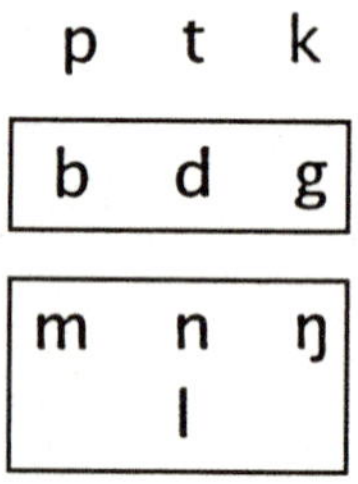

6. Provide a feature matrix for each of the following sounds.

   a. [ð θ f v]

   b. [g ʤ]

   c. [u o]

   d. [i ɪ e ɛ æ]

DERIVATIONS

Derivations are a representation of how phonemes and allophones are related. Phonetic forms are derived from phonemic forms by applying phonological processes in the form of a rule. There are three parts to a derivation. These parts are very similar to the components of a phonological rule.

⇒ **Underlying Representation (UR).** The underlying representation is a representation of native speaker knowledge and is always in phonemic transcription.

⇒ **Rules.** Remember that phonemes and allophones are linked by a rule. The rule applies to change the phoneme into the allophone. This, of course, only occurs when the structural description (environment) specified in the rule is found in the underlying representation.

⇒ **Phonetic Representation (PR).** The phonetic representation is also called the surface representation. Since the surface representation always represents pronunciation, it is in phonetic transcription.

An example....

In English, liquids (and glides) become voiceless after a voiceless stop at the beginning of a syllable. This is an example of devoicing and can be captured with a rule such as:

Liquid/Glide Devoicing:

$$\begin{bmatrix} \text{-syllabic} \\ \text{+sonorant} \\ \text{+voice} \\ \text{-nasal} \end{bmatrix} \rightarrow [\text{-voice}] \;/\; \sigma \begin{bmatrix} \text{-syllabic} \\ \text{+consonantal} \\ \text{-continuant} \\ \text{-voice} \\ \text{-delayed release} \end{bmatrix} \underline{\qquad}$$

- The first feature matrix captures the class of liquids.
- The second part of the rule captures the change in voicing that occurs.
- The third part of the rule captures that the process only applies after a voiceless stop at the beginning of a syllable. Recall that σ is used to indicate a syllable.

The derivation below illustrates how the phonetic form is derived from the phonological form using this rule.

UR	# pliz #	'please'	# læf #	'laugh'
Liquid/Glide Devoicing	# pl̥iz #		———	
PR	[pl̥iz]		[læf]	

- In the word *please*, Liquid/Glide Devoicing applies because [l] occurs after a voiceless consonant (i.e., [p]). The structural description of the rule has been met. Notice that after the rule has applied, [l] has become voiceless (i.e., [l̥]).

- In the word *laugh*, the rule does not apply as indicated by the dashed line, since the structural description necessary for the rule to apply was not met: [l] occurs at the beginning of the word and not after a voiceless consonant. The phonetic form, therefore, remains the same as the underlying form.

See **Figure 3.14** on **pg. 94** of the text for an example of a derivation involving aspiration and vowel lengthening in English.

RULE ORDERING

More than one rule can apply during the derivation of a particular form. Sometimes the order in which rules apply is crucial to deriving the appropriate phonetic form. That is, one rule must apply before another. An example involves the rule of liquid devoicing (from page 67) and the rule of schwa deletion presented below.

Schwa Deletion: $[\text{ə}] \rightarrow \emptyset \;/\; C_0 \underline{\qquad\qquad} \sigma\; C_0 \underset{[+\text{stress}]}{V}$

- The first and second parts of the rule refer to the deletion of schwa.
- The third part of the rule captures that this occurs only when schwa is in an open syllable followed by a stressed syllable. The first C_0 represents any number of successive onset consonants from zero up that may occur before schwa. σ represents the syllable boundary, and the second C_0 again represents any onset consonants that may occur before the stressed vowel of the next syllable.

The Incorrect Order ... Schwa Deletion must apply before Liquid/Glide Devoicing. If Liquid/Glide Devoicing is applied before schwa deletion, then liquids incorrectly remain voiced in the phonetic form. This is shown in the following derivation of the word 'police'.

UR	# pəlís # 'police'
Liquid/Glide Devoicing	———
Schwa Deletion	# plís #
PR	[plís]

(**Note:** It is assumed that stress placement has already occurred. Normally, stress would not be present in the underlying form because it is predictable in English, and therefore would be applied using a stress rule.)

The Correct Order ... Since liquids in English are produced without voice following a voiceless stop, schwa deletion must occur first so that in the resulting output, liquids occur after voiceless stops, creating the necessary environment for Liquid/Glide Devoicing to apply.

UR	# pəlís #	'police'
Schwa Deletion	# plís #	
Liquid/Glide Devoicing	# pl̥ís #	
PR	[pl̥ís]	

As shown in the above derivation, the phonetic form now contains, as it should in English, a voiceless liquid!

QUICK REMINDER!

Underlying representations capture the phonological knowledge speakers have about the contrastive sounds of their language. Therefore, these representations are always in phonemic transcription, which does not contain any predictable phonetic information.

Since surface representations capture actual phonetic outputs, they are always in phonetic transcription. That is, they contain all of the predictable phonetic information not found in the underlying representation.

Processes, in the form of rules, apply to add predictable phonetic information to the underlying representation, thereby creating the surface representation!

EVEN MORE PHONOLOGY PROBLEMS!

For each data set:

- determine if the sounds are allophones of the same phoneme, allophones of separate phonemes, or in free variation. Remember to provide evidence in support of your conclusion along with a representation of the phoneme(s).
- for all allophones of the same phoneme, provide a rule. Wherever possible, try to write one rule for all the sounds you have investigated. HINT … watch out for natural classes!
- for all allophones of the same phoneme involving natural classes, write a rule using feature notation.
- for all allophones of the same phoneme, identify the articulatory process that your rule describes.
- provide derivations as indicated.

1. Canadian French: [t] and [ts]

[ts]	This symbol represents a voiceless alveolar affricate
[y]	This symbol represents a high front tense rounded vowel
[ʏ]	This symbol represents a high front lax rounded vowel

1. [tu]	all	7. [telegram]	telegram
2. [abutsi]	ended	8. [trɛ]	very
3. [tɛl]	such	9. [kyltsyr]	culture
4. [tab]	stamp	10. [minʏt]	minute
5. [tsimɪd]	timid	11. [tsy]	you
6. [tsɪt]	title	12. [tsʏb]	tube

- provide a derivation for #5, #10, and #12

2. Burmese: [m] and [m̥], [n] and [n̥], [ŋ] and [ŋ̥]

Hint: Given that you have been asked to investigate three sets of nasals, would you expect all the nasals to pattern in the same way?

1. [mi]	five	8. [hm̥i]	to lean against
2. [mwej]	to give birth	9. [hm̥wej]	fragrant
3. [mjiʔ]	river	10. [hm̥jajʔ]	to cure
4. [ne]	small	11. [hn̥ej]	slow
5. [nwe]	to bend	12. [hŋ̥a]	to lend property
6. [ŋa]	five	13. [hn̥wej]	to heat
7. [ŋouʔ]	tree stump	14. [hŋ̥eʔ]	bird

- provide a derivation for #3, #9, and #13

3. Malay: [t] and [tʲ]

[ʲ] This diacritic represents a sound that has been palatalized.

1. [tarek]	pull	6. [tʲampah]	tasteless
2. [kətʲut]	shriveled	7. [kətil]	pinch
3. [pitər]	disk	8. [tʲarek]	rip
4. [ʧomel]	cute	9. [lawat]	visit
5. [batʲa]	steel	10. [ʧampah]	tasteless

- Look at the Malay data again and examine [tʲ] and [ʧ]. What conclusion can you make about these two sounds? Give evidence to support your answer.

4. Tamil: [p] and [b], [k] and [g], [ṭ] and [ḍ], [t̪] and [d̪]

[̣] This diacritic means that a sound is retroflex.
[̪] This diacritic means that a sound is dental.
[ɨ] This symbol represents a high central unrounded vowel.

Remember: When looking for complementary distribution, you must record the immediate surrounding phonetic environment around EACH OCCURRENCE of a sound.

1. [pal] tooth
2. [abayam] refuge
3. [kappal] ship
4. [saabam] curse
5. [kaakkaaj] crow
6. [mugil] cloud
7. [t̪ugil] veil
8. [t̪aṭṭɨ] plate
9. [padɨ] lie down
10. [t̪uukkɨ] carry
11. [id̪ɨ] this
12. [ad̪ɨ] that
13. [kat̪t̪i] knife
14. [kud̪i] jump
15. [pat̪t̪i] ten
16. [paad̪am] foot
17. [iḍam] place
18. [kaaṭpaaḍi] name of a town
19. [paṭṭɨ] silk

- provide a derivation for #3, #6, and #14

5. Igbirra: [e] and [a]

1. [mezi] I expect
2. [meze] I am well
3. [meto] I arrange
4. [metu] I beat
5. [mazɪ] I am in pain
6. [mazɛ] I agree
7. [matɔ] I pick
8. [matʊ] I send

- Are there minimal pairs?
- [e] and [a] both occur between m _ z and m _ t. What significance does this have for your analysis?

6. Gascon: [b] and [β], [d] and [ð], [g] and [ɣ]

Hint: Think about what process you would expect given pairs of stops and fricatives.

[ɣ] This symbol represents a voiced velar fricative.

1.	[brẽn]	endanger	10.	[ʒuɣɛt]	he played
2.	[dilys]	Monday	11.	[krãmbo]	room
3.	[taldepãn]	leftover bread	12.	[eʃaðo]	hoe
4.	[ʃiβaw]	horse	13.	[gat]	cat
5.	[pũnde]	to lay eggs	14.	[aβe]	to have
6.	[agro]	sour	15.	[biɣar]	mosquito
7.	[puðe]	to be able	16.	[ũmbro]	shadow
8.	[riɣut]	he laughed	17.	[dudze]	twelve
9.	[noβi]	husband	18.	[lũŋg]	long

- Examine the Gascon data again, paying attention to the oral and nasal vowels. Can you make any conclusions about nasalized vowels in this language? Write one statement involving classes of sounds, describing their behavior.

- Provide a derivation for #3, #9, #12, and #16. Do your rules need to be ordered? Why or why not?

REMINDER ... REMINDER ...

To solve a phonology problem, you must have a firm grasp on minimal pairs, near minimal pairs, complementary distribution, and phonemes and allophones. If you don't, then you need to get some help!

REVIEW! REVIEW! Make sure you can:

- define phonemes and allophones
- spot minimal and near minimal pairs
- find free variation
- determine complementary distribution
- construct representations of phonemes
- construct syllable representations
- identify consonantal and vowel features
- put together feature matrices
- put together rules
- put together rules using feature notation
- construct derivations
- solve phonology problems

QUESTIONS? PROBLEMS? DIFFICULTIES?

CHAPTER 4. MORPHOLOGY: THE ANALYSIS OF WORD STRUCTURE

Morphology is the study of words: their categories, their internal structure, and the operations that form them. Some of the important topics and concepts found in this chapter include:

1. morphological terminology
2. identifying morphemes
3. identifying lexical categories
4. analyzing word structure
5. derivation
6. compounding
7. inflection
8. other morphological processes
9. morphology problems
10. morphophonemics

MORPHOLOGICAL TERMINOLOGY

The following terms are crucial to understanding morphology. You should know them!

TERM	DEFINITION
Word	Words are the smallest free-forms found in language. Free-forms are elements which can appear in isolation, or whose position is not fixed. Words can be simple or complex. See **Table 4.1** on **pg. 111** of the text for some examples.
Morpheme	A morpheme is the smallest meaning or functional unit found in language. Morphemes can be free or bound.
Allomorphs	Allomorphs are the different forms of a morpheme.
Root	A root is the core of a word. It is the portion of the word that carries most of the word's meaning. The majority of English words are built from roots that are free morphemes, making English a word-based language. Some English words, though, are built from roots that are bound morphemes. Think of some examples.
Affixes	Affixes are different types of bound morphemes. There are three types of affixes found in language: prefixes, suffixes, and infixes. See **Tables 4.3** and **4.4** on **pg. 114** of the text for some examples.
Base	A base is any form to which an affix is added. The base may be the same as the root, but it can also be larger than the root. See **Figure 4.3** on **pg. 113** of the text for an illustration of the difference between roots and bases.

IDENTIFYING MORPHEMES

Morphemes are the building blocks of words. A word may contain only one morpheme, making it a simple word, or a word may contain more than one morpheme, making it a complex word. Below are some hints for determining the number of morphemes that a word contains.

⇒ A morpheme carries information about meaning or function. Think.... can the word *haunt* be divided into the morphemes *h* and *aunt*? To do so, both *h* and *aunt* must have meaning. Do they? What about the word *bats*? What meaning does *s* have in this word?

⇒ The meanings of individual morphemes should contribute to the overall meaning of the word. Think.... can the word pumpkin be divided into the morphemes *pump* and *kin*? To do so, the meaning of *pumpkin* must have something to do with the meaning of both *pump* and *kin*. Does it?

⇒ A morpheme is not the same as a syllable. A morpheme can consist of one or more syllables, but a morpheme does not have to be a syllable. Think... how many syllables are found in the morpheme *treat*? What about in the morpheme *Dracula*? What about the s found in *bats*? It is a morpheme, but is it a syllable?

⇒ Often as words are built, changes in pronunciation and/or spelling occur. These do not affect a morpheme's status as a morpheme. Think.... when *y* is added to the morpheme *scare*, it becomes *scary*, and when *er* is added to *scary*, it becomes *scarier*. Is the root the same in both *scary* and *scarier*? Is the root *scare* or *scar*? What is the base for *scary*? What about in *scarier*? Is the base the same in both?

Identify the number of morphemes in each of the following words.

insert	____________	supply	____________
memory	____________	supplies	____________
		supplier	____________
format	____________	faster	____________
flowchart	____________	power	____________
bug	____________	processor	____________
debug	____________		

MORPHEMES! MORPHEMES!

For each of the following words, identify the number of morphemes and write the free and bound morphemes in the appropriate blanks. A free morpheme can be a word by itself, while a bound morpheme must be attached to another element. Remember, a word may have more than one bound morpheme. The first is done for you.

WORD	TOTAL # OF MORPHEMES	FREE	BOUND
eraser	2	erase	-er
wicked	________	________	________
invalid (A)	________	________	________
invalid (N)	________	________	________
Jack's	________	________	________
optionality	________	________	________
refurnish	________	________	________
inabilities	________	________	________
denationalize	________	________	________
present	________	________	________
activation	________	________	________

Think .... What type of bound morpheme is found in the complex words *optionality* and *activation*? Prefix? Suffix? Infix? Remember for an affix to be an infix, it must be found inside another morpheme and not between two morphemes.

IDENTIFYING LEXICAL CATEGORIES

In morphology, we are concerned with four lexical categories: nouns, verbs, adjectives, and prepositions. Nouns typically refer to people and things (both concrete and abstract). Verbs typically denote actions, sensations, and states. Adjectives usually name properties. Prepositions generally encode spatial relations.

For each of the words below, state the number of morphemes found in the word, and identify the root, the lexical category of the root, and the lexical category of the entire word. Remember, the root is the core of the word and carries most of the word's meaning. Be careful: the root's lexical category and the word's lexical category may or may not be the same. The first is done for you.

WORD	# OF MORPHS	ROOT	ROOT CATEGORY	WORD CATEGORY
kindnesses	3	kind	adjective	noun
amazement	____	__________	__________	__________
reusable	____	__________	__________	__________
dishonest	____	__________	__________	__________
Calgary	____	__________	__________	__________
lovelier	____	__________	__________	__________
historical	____	__________	__________	__________
uncontrolled	____	__________	__________	__________
impersonal	____	__________	__________	__________
trees	____	__________	__________	__________
faster	____	__________	__________	__________
rereads	____	__________	__________	__________
beautiful	____	__________	__________	__________
child	____	__________	__________	__________

WORD TREES

A word tree is a representation of a word's internal structure. To put together a word tree you need to be able to determine the number of morphemes in a word, identify roots and affixes, and assign lexical categories. Remember, prefixes are attached to the front of a base, while suffixes are attached to the end of a base. Infixes are a type of affix that occurs inside another morpheme; they are not found in English.

Below are some examples of how to draw a word tree.

1. Words with a single affix.

a) Root + Suffix

1. Identify the root and determine its lexical category

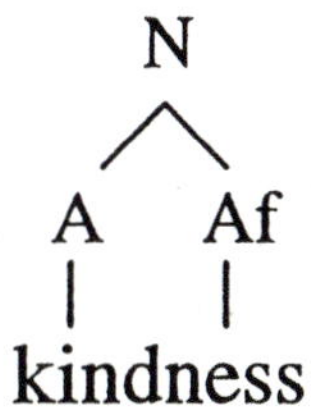

2. Attach the suffix and determine the lexical category of the resulting word. This may or may not be the same as the lexical category of the root.

b) Prefix + Root

1. Identify the root and determine its lexical category

2. Attach the prefix and determine the lexical category of the resulting word. This is typically the same as the lexical category of the root.

2. Words with multiple suffixes.

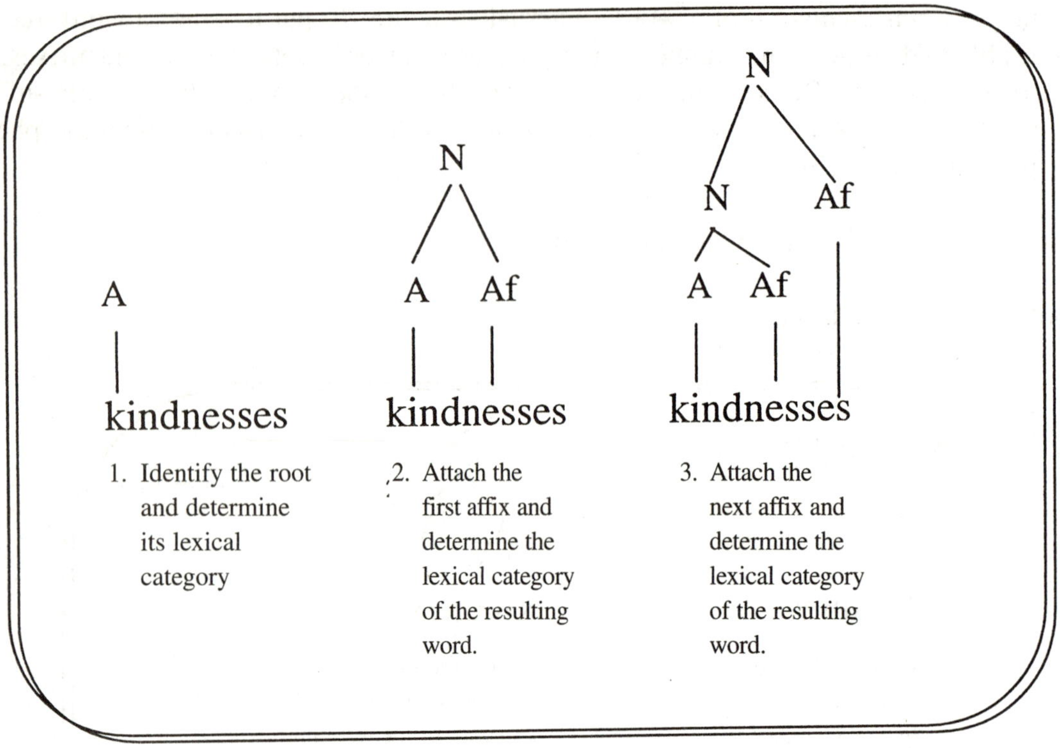

3. Words with both a prefix and a suffix.

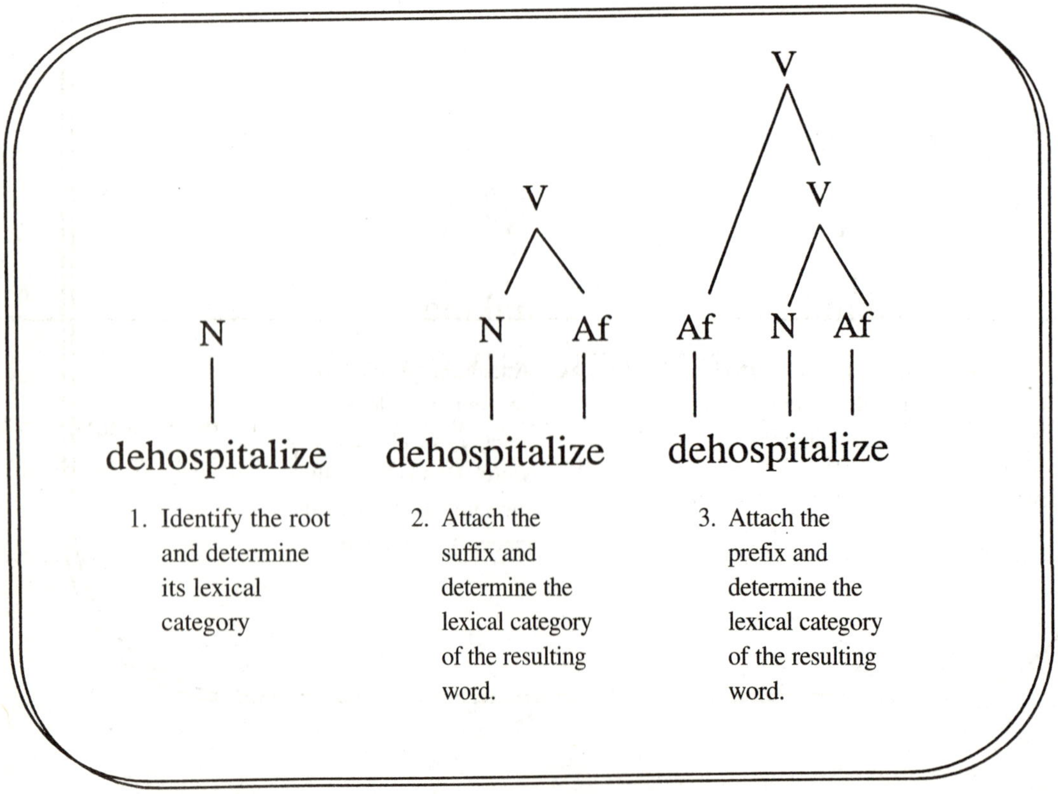

4. Words that are structurally ambiguous.

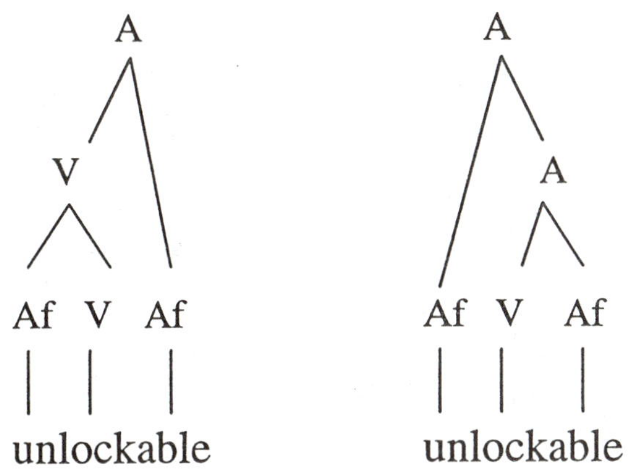

The prefix 'un' is first attached to create the verb 'unlock'. The suffix 'able' is then attached to create the adjective 'unlockable'.

The suffix 'able' is first attached to create the adjective 'lockable'. The prefix 'un' is then attached to create the adjective 'unlockable'.

Exercise! Exercise! To practice, draw trees for the following words:

- trees
- lovelier
- dishonest
- beautiful
- amazement
- reusable
- impersonal
- Calgary

REMINDER! REMINDER!

To be able to draw word trees correctly, you need to be able to identify nouns, verbs, adjectives, and prepositions. If you are having difficulty with these, refer to **Chapter 5 section 5.1** of the text to get some help!

DERIVATION

Derivation is a process of affixation. Affixation is a morphological process which adds affixes to words. Derivational affixes are affixes which build a word having a different (but usually related) meaning from of the base. The resulting word may also belong to a different lexical category from its base.

⇒ English has many derivational suffixes. These suffixes typically cause both a meaning and category change to the base. For example:

- -ity combines with an adjective such as 'stupid' to create the noun 'stupidity', meaning the result of being 'stupid'.

- -ful combines with a noun such as 'faith' to create the adjective 'faithful', meaning having 'faith'.

- -ment combines with a verb such as 'adjourn' to create the noun 'adjournment', meaning the result of 'adjourning'.

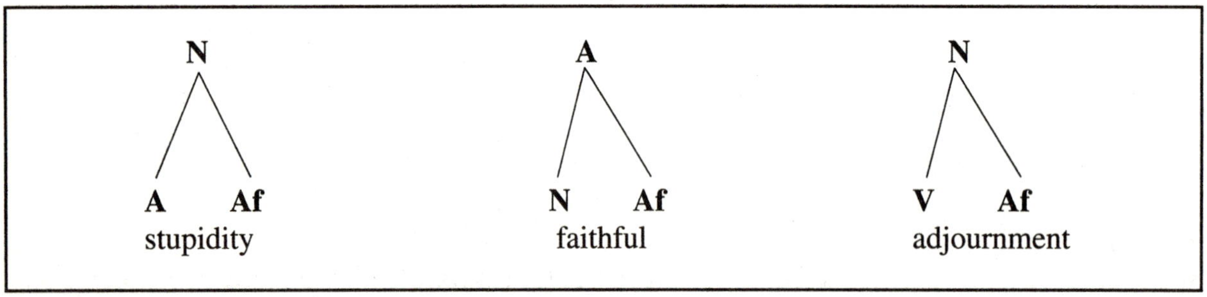

Think of some more derivational suffixes. What lexical category of words do they combine with? What lexical category of words do they create?

⇒ English also has many derivational prefixes; however, these do not usually change the lexical category of the base. They do cause a meaning change to the base. For this reason, English prefixes are still considered derivational. For example:

- re- combines with a verb such as 'think' to create the verb 'rethink', meaning to think again.

- in- combines with an adjective such as 'complete' to create the adjective 'incomplete', meaning not complete.

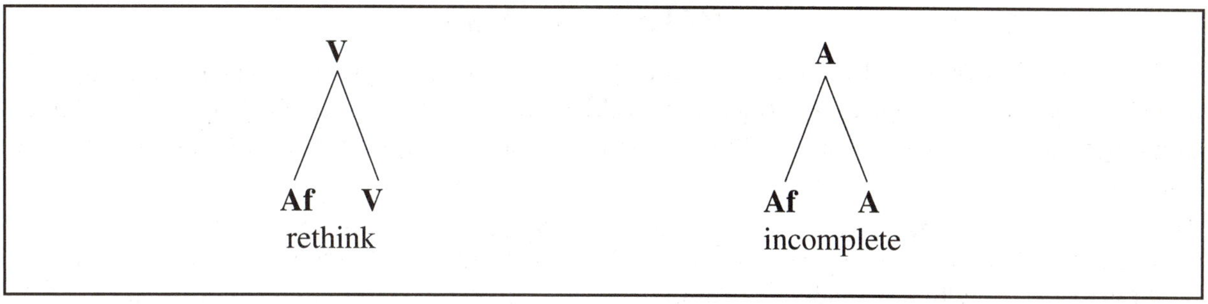

Think of some more derivational prefixes. What lexical category of words do they combine with and create? What meaning change occurs to the base when these are added?

More examples of English derivational prefixes and suffixes can be found in **Table 4.6** on **pg. 117** of the text.

⇒ Derivational affixes (including those found in English) are often subject to restrictions. For example:

- Derivational affixes combine with bases of particular lexical categories.
  e.g., -ize must be attached to a noun / -er must be attached to a verb

- Derivational affixes combine with bases having certain phonological properties.
  e.g., -en must be attached to a base having one syllable and ending in an obstruent

- Derivational affixes combine with bases of specific linguistic origin.
  e.g., -ant must be attached to a base of Latin origin

⇒ English has two types of derivational affixes. Class 1 affixes often cause changes to the consonant or vowel sounds in the base. Class 2 affixes do not. Class 1 affixes may also cause changes to which syllable is stressed. Class 2 affixes do not. See **Tables 4.9** and **4.10** on **pg. 120** of the text for examples of both types of English derivational affixes.

Try this! Draw trees for the following words. Remember that a word can contain more than one derivational affix.

- disappear
- homeless
- electricity
- unbreakable
- instituitional
- lodger

Now... go back over the above words and identify which affixes are Class I affixes and which belong to Class 2.

COMPOUNDING

Compounding is another process used to build words. Compounding involves the combination of two or more already existing words into a new word. Most English compounds are nouns, verbs, and adjectives.

There are four important concepts about English compounds that you should know.

⇒ **Headedness.** The head of a compound is the morpheme that determines the category of the entire compound. Most English compounds are right-headed. That is, the category of the entire compound is the same as the category of the rightmost member of the compound. For example, since the rightmost member *board* is a noun, the compound *blackboard* is a noun.

⇒ **Stress Patterns.** Even though compounds can be spelled as one word, two words, or with a hyphen separating the morphemes, a generalization can be made about the stress patterns found on them. Stress tends to be more prominent on the first member of the compound rather than the second: for example, *greénhouse* (a garden centre) versus *green hoúse* (a house that is green).

⇒ **Tense/Plural.** Tense and plural markers are usually added to the compound as a whole and not to the first member of the compound. For example, the plural of *fire engine* is *fire engines* and not *fires engine*. What is the past tense of *drop kick*?

⇒ **Meaning Relationships.** Compounds can be classified as either endocentric or exocentric. This classification is based on the meaning relationship between the members of the compound. In an endocentric compound, the entire compound denotes a subtype of the head. For example, a *tea-cup* is a type of *cup*, and a *lunch-room* is a type of *room*. In an exocentric compound, the meaning of the compound does not come from the head. For example, a *redneck* is not a type of *neck*, but a type of person.

Compounds can be formed from smaller compounds. As well, compounding can be used in conjunction with derivation to build words. For example, the compound *blackboard* can combine with the derived word *eraser* to create the larger compound *blackboard eraser*.

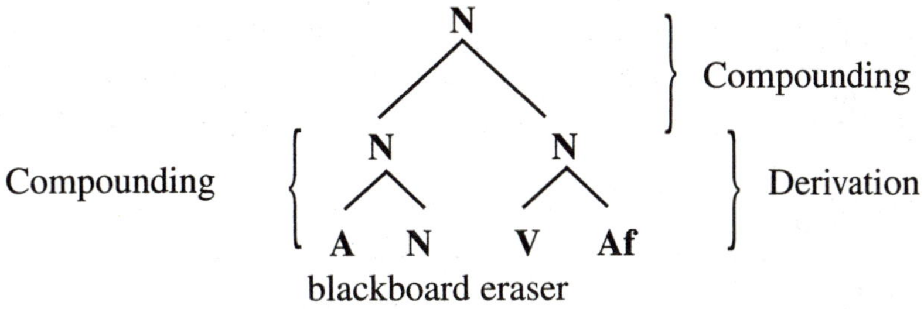

EXERCISE!

For each compound below, state the lexical categories making it up and give another example of that type of compound. The first is done for you.

COMPOUND	LEXICAL CATEGORIES	EXAMPLE
bathroom	Noun + Noun	movie star
scarecrow	____________	____________
skin-deep	____________	____________
bittersweet	____________	____________
upstairs	____________	____________

Now... go back and draw a word tree for each compound. **Then...** draw a word tree for each of the following compounds.

- (an) undertaking
- washer-dryer
- presidential election
- lighthouse keeper

INFLECTION

Inflection involves modifying the form of a word to indicate grammatical information such as singular versus plural or past versus non-past.

Inflection is most commonly a process of affixation. Inflectional affixes do not change the lexical category of the base.

⇒ English has eight inflectional affixes. These are found on nouns, verbs, and adjectives and provide the following grammatical information: plural (*-s*) and possessive (*-'s*); third person singular non-past tense (*-s*), past tense (*-ed*), progressive (*-ing*) and past participle (*-en*/*-ed*); comparative (*-er*) and superlative (*-est*).

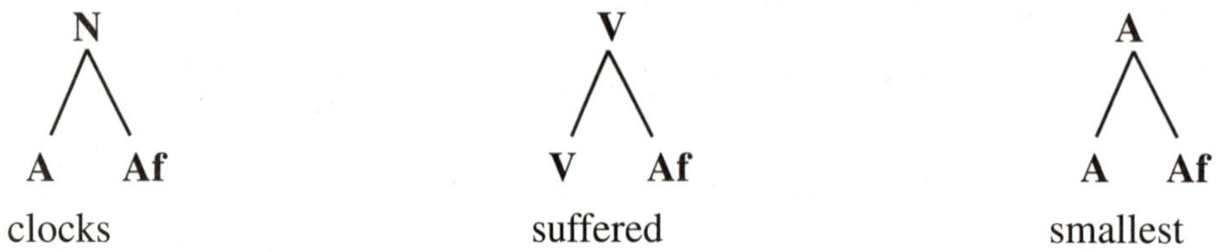

See **Table 4.5** on **pg. 125** of the text for some examples of English inflectional affixes.

Practice! For each of the following words, identify the lexical category of the root and the type of inflectional information found (i.e., past tense, superlative, plural, etc.). The first is done for you.

WORD	LEXICAL CATEGORY	INFLECTIONAL INFORMATION
1. watched	verb	past tense
2. runs		
3. sorriest		
4. lamps		
5. playing		
6. driven		
7. lovelier		

INFLECTION VERSUS DERIVATION

It can sometimes be hard to determine whether an affix is an inflectional affix or a derivational affix. The boxes below provide some criteria for helping determine whether an affix is inflectional or derivational.

Inflectional affixes ...

- do not change the lexical category or meaning of the base.
- occur after derivational affixes have been attached.
- are productive, meaning there are relatively few exceptions on the class of bases to which they can attach.
- are semantically transparent, meaning that it is easy to determine the contribution of the affix to the meaning of the resulting word.

Derivational affixes ...

- typically change both the lexical category and meaning of the base.
- occur closer to the root than inflectional affixes.
- are less productive than inflectional affixes, meaning there are restrictions on the class of bases to which they can attach.
- are less semantically transparent than inflectional affixes, meaning that it is not always easy to determine the contribution of the affix to the meaning of the resulting word.

Identify the Affix! Each of the following English words contains at least one affix. For each word, identify all the affixes, and for each affix state whether it is inflectional (IA) or derivational (DA). The first is done for you.

WORD	AFFIX(ES)	IA / DA
trucks	-s	IA (plural)
instructional	____________	____________
reuse	____________	____________
girl's	____________	____________
smaller	____________	____________
delightful	____________	____________
nationalize	____________	____________
watched	____________	____________
mistreat	____________	____________
unhealthiest	____________	____________

It can get even more complicated! Many affixes have the same form but can be either inflectional or derivational, or they can be different inflectional or different derivational affixes. To correctly identify an affix as inflectional or derivational, you need to pay attention to how the affix is functioning in the word rather than its form. Use the four criteria outlined in this section to help you decide if an affix is functioning as an inflectional affix or a derivational affix.

Form versus Function! In each group of four words below, two words have affixes of the same type, one word has a different affix, and one word has no affix at all. Next to each word, write S (same), D (different), or N (none) based on the other words in the data set. You may want to use a dictionary. The first is done for you.

1. ovens ___S___
   lens ___N___
   hens ___S___
   listens ___D___

2. greener ______
   farmer ______
   colder ______
   water ______

3. greedy ______
   ivory ______
   jealousy ______
   dirty ______

4. friendly ______
   slowly ______
   intelligently ______
   early ______

5. leaven ______
   harden ______
   spoken ______
   thicken ______

6. intelligent ______
   inhale ______
   incongruous ______
   inhuman ______

7. rider ______
   colder ______
   silver ______
   actor ______

8. candied ______
   shopped ______
   cleaned ______
   candid ______

REMINDER!

Many more inflectional phenomena, including case and agreement, are widely used in language. For more information on these, visit www.pearsoned.ca/ogrady (the access code for the website comes with your copy of the sixth edition). Select chapter 4, "More on inflection."

PRACTICE WITH WORD TREES

Draw one tree for each of the words listed below and identify whether inflection, derivation, and/or compounding was used to build the word. Remember that more than one process can be used in a single word. Use the context sentence to help you determine the lexical category of the entire word!

For example, the word ***unfixable*** might be diagrammed as follows.

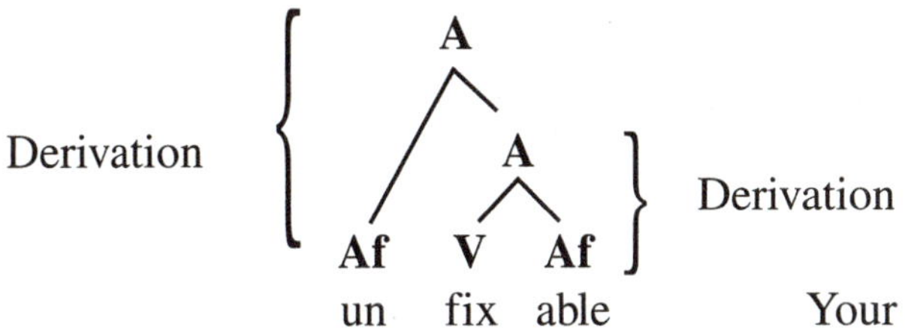

Your car is unfixable.

	WORD	CONTEXT SENTENCE
1.	taken	The baby has taken his first steps.
2.	spoonfeeding	Mother is spoonfeeding the baby.
3.	softest	The softest pillow has the
4.	silkiest	silkiest cover.
5.	introductions	Mary performed the introductions.
6.	steps	John steps up the ladder.
7.	steps	I hate those steep steps.
8.	stringier	My hair is stringier than hers.
9.	skiers	The skiers were rich.

10. father — My father lives in France.
11. stone-cold — Your french-fries are stone-cold.
12. making — Jill is making candy.
13. boxing — We watched the boxing.
14. criticize — You criticize too much.
15. creamy — Creamy chocolate is delicious.
16. keepers — The keepers locked up.
17. blessing — Give me your blessing.
18. blessing — She is blessing the bread.
19. school teacher — My mother was a school teacher.
20. clumsiness — I detest clumsiness.
21. windmills — Holland has lots of windmills.
22. hammered — John hammered on the door.
23. thickeners — There are many different types of thickeners.
24. unlocked — We unlocked the door.
25. declaw — You should declaw your cat.
26. retry — She should retry the recipe.
27. inside — The cat is inside the box.
28. impure — Impure water is dangerous.
29. sleepwalking — George is often found sleepwalking.
30. defrosting — The steaks are defrosting.

> **QUICK REMINDER!**
>
> Remember that ALL English prefixes are derivational even though they do not cause a lexical category change!

INFLECTIONAL PROCESSES

In addition to affixation, inflection can also be marked using internal change, suppletion, reduplication and tone placement.

PROCESS	DEFINITION
Internal Change	This process provides grammatical information by substituting a portion of the morpheme. In English, the tense of a word can be marked by replacing the vowel with another vowel (e.g., run → ran). See **Table 4.17** on **pg. 128** of the text for more examples.
Suppletion	This process provides grammatical information by replacing one morpheme with an entirely different morpheme. In English, the tense of a word can be marked in this way (e.g., go → went). See **Table 4.18** on **pg. 129** of the text for more examples. Partial suppletion is sometimes used to describe the change in words such as think → thought in which more than a segment has been changed, but not the entire morpheme.
Reduplication	A process which repeats all (full) or a portion (partial) of the base to mark a semantic or grammatical contrast. This process is not productive in English. See **Tables 4.19** and **4.20** on **pg. 130** of the text for some international examples.
Tone Placement	This process is found in tone languages where differences in tone can be used to mark grammatical information such as a change in tense or number. See **Table 4.21** on **pg. 131** of the text for some examples from Mono-Bili (spoken in the Congo).

Exercise! Exercise! Each of the following words has been inflected. For each, identify the type of inflectional process that has been used to mark the grammatical contrast. The first has been done for you.

WORD	**TYPE OF INFLECTION**
drove	internal change
was	____________________
(is) jumping	____________________

anak anak
'all sorts of children' ______________________

better ______________________

lovelier ______________________

George's ______________________

tatakbuh
'will run' ______________________

mice ______________________

OTHER MORPHOLOGICAL PROCESSES

PROCESS	DEFINITION
Cliticization	Clitics are morphemes that behave like words in terms of meaning and function. Clitics differ, though, in that they cannot stand alone as a word. Cliticization attaches these elements to either the beginning of a following word or the end of a preceding word. e.g., 're' from 'are' is attached to 'they', as in they're
Conversion	A process which assigns an existing word to a different lexical category. The lexical category and meaning change that occur make this process a type of derivation. e.g., butter (N) → (to) butter (V) See **Table 4.22** on **pg. 132** of the text for more examples. Conversion can also be accompanied by a change in stress placement. See **Table 4.23** on **pg. 132** of the text for some examples.
Clipping	A process which shortens a polysyllabic word by removing one or more syllables. e.g., condominium → condo
Blends	A process which creates a new word by combining non-morphemic portions of two existing words. e.g., spiced + ham → spam

Backformation	A process which creates a word by removing a real or supposed affix from an existing word in the language. e.g., enthuse ← enthusiasm See **Table 4.24** on **pg. 134** of the text for more English examples.
Acronyms	A process which creates new words using the initial letters of the words in a phrase or title and pronouncing them as a word. e.g., scuba, UNICEF Acronyms are different from Initialisms, in which each letter making up the word is pronounced. e.g., IBM, NHL
Onomatopoeia	Words that have been created to sound like the thing they name. e.g., buzz, hiss, sizzle See **Table 4.25** on **pg. 135** of the text for some examples across languages.

Other ways to form new words include:

- Word Manufacture (Coinage), in which a totally new word is created. This process commonly occurs with product names.
- Creating words from names (called eponyms). See **Table 4.26** on **pg. 135** of the text for some examples.
- Borrowing words from other languages.

Practice! Practice! Identify the process responsible for formation of each of the following English words. Choose any of the morphological phenomena from the above table as well as inflection, derivation, and compounding. The first is done for you.

1. infomercial blending
2. (to) ship ______________________
3. mice ______________________
4. support-hose ______________________
5. chirp ______________________
6. MADD ______________________

7. healthy ______________________________

8. demo ______________________________

9. sadness ______________________________

10. he's ______________________________

11. head-line ______________________________

12. beep ______________________________

13. ATM ______________________________

14. jumped ______________________________

There are many examples of different word formation processes in the following passage. Find all the examples of ACRONYM, BACKFORMATION, BLENDING, CLIPPING, COINAGE, COMPOUNDING, and INITIALISM.

> John didn't enthuse about UCLA, as he probably expected his profs to spoon feed him. He preferred to avoid the smog by taking sandwiches to the beach where he would laze around and go scuba diving in his new dacron dry suit. One day he was suffering from a headache and dizziness, which he thought might be caused by sunstroke or the flu, so he went to the doctor. The doc sent him to the lab for a urinalysis and a blood test and suggested that he should see an ENT specialist as well. He is now OK, having returned from the USA, and he is learning about ohms, watts, and volts at MIT.

Get ready for morphology problems ...

INTRODUCTION TO MORPHOLOGY PROBLEMS

The goal in morphology problems is to isolate and identify all the morphemes in the data given. To do this, you must identify recurring strings of sounds and match them with recurring meanings. Here are a few easy ones to try!

All data is given in phonetic transcription.

1. Mende (Sierra Leone)

1.	[pɛlɛ]	house	9.	[pɛlɛi]	the house
2.	[mɔm]	glass	10.	[mɔmi]	the glass
3.	[dɔmi]	story	11.	[dɔmii]	the story
4.	[kali]	hoe	12.	[kalii]	the hoe
5.	[hele]	elephant	13.	[helei]	the elephant
6.	[kaamɔ]	teacher	14.	[kaamɔi]	the teacher
7.	[navo]	boy	15.	[navoi]	the boy
8.	[numu]	person	16.	[numui]	the person

a. What is the morpheme meaning 'the'?

b. Given [sale] meaning 'proverb', what is the form for 'the proverb'?

c. If [kpindii] means 'the night', then what does [kpindi] mean?

2. Ganada (Uganda)

1.	[omukazi]	woman	6.	[abakazi]	women
2.	[omusawo]	doctor	7.	[abasawo]	doctors
3.	[omusika]	heir	8.	[abasika]	heirs
4.	[omuwala]	girl	9.	[abawala]	girls
5.	[omulenzi]	boy	10.	[abalenzi]	boys

a. What is the morpheme meaning 'singular'?

b. What is the morpheme meaning 'plural'?

c. Given [abalanga] meaning 'twins', what would the form be for 'twin'?

3. Kanuri (Nigeria)

1. [gana]	small	6. [nəmgana]	smallness
2. [kura]	big	7. [nəmkura]	bigness
3. [kurugu]	long	8. [nəmkurugu]	length
4. [karite]	excellent	9. [nəmkarite]	excellence
5. [dibi]	bad	10. [nəmdibi]	badness

a. What type of affix is shown (i.e., prefix, suffix, infix)?

b. What is the affix?

c. Given [kəji] meaning 'sweet', what is the form for 'sweetness'?

d. Given [nəmgəla] meaning 'goodness', what is the form for 'good'?

e. What morphological process was used to form the words in the second column?

f. Draw a word-tree for [nəmkurugu] 'length'.

REMINDER

For more tips on identifying morphemes in unfamiliar languages (i.e., solving morphology problems), see **pgs. 137** and **138** of the text.

MORE MORPHOLOGY PROBLEMS

The following pages contain a number of data sets from different languages. These data sets are intended to give you practice in doing morphological analysis. Each contains sufficient data to make valid conclusions; however, the data may have been regularized somewhat. All data is in phonetic transcription.

1. Turkish

1.	[deniz]	an ocean	9.	[elim]	my hand
2.	[denize]	to an ocean	10.	[eller]	hands
3.	[denizin]	of an ocean	11.	[disler]	teeth
4.	[eve]	to a house	12.	[disimizin]	of our tooth
5.	[evden]	from a house	13.	[dislerimizin]	of our teeth
6.	[evcikden]	from a little house	14.	[elcike]	to a little hand
7.	[denizcikde]	in a little ocean	15.	[denizlerimizde]	in our oceans
8.	[elde]	in a hand	16.	[evciklerimizde]	in our little houses

Give the Turkish morpheme which corresponds to each of the following English translations.

ocean	________________	my	________________
house	________________	our	________________
hand	________________	of	________________
tooth	________________	little	________________
plural	________________	from	________________
to	________________	in	________________

What is the order of morphemes in a Turkish word in terms of noun, preposition, plural, possessive determiner and adjective? (Don't assume that this order will be the same as it is in English.)

What would be the Turkish word meaning 'of our little hands'? (HINT: use the order you determined above.)

2. Bontoc (Philippines)

1. [fikas]	strong	5. [fumikas]	he is becoming strong
2. [kilad]	red	6. [kumilad]	he is becoming red
3. [bato]	stone	7. [bumato]	he is becoming stone
4. [fusul]	enemy	8. [fumusul]	he is becoming an enemy

What is the affix used to form the verbs?

What type of affix (i.e., prefix, suffix, infix) is used to form the verbs?

What morphological process is used to build the verbs?

3. Michoacan Aztec (also known as Nahuatl—Mexico)

1. [nokali]	my house	8. [mopelo]	your dog
2. [nokalimes]	my houses	9. [mopelomes]	your dogs
3. [mokali]	your house	10. [ipelo]	his dog
4. [ikali]	his house	11. [nokwahmili]	my cornfield
5. [kali]	house	12. [mokwahmili]	your cornfield
6. [kalimes]	houses	13. [ikwahmili]	his cornfield
7. [nopelo]	my dog	14. [ikwahmilimes]	his cornfields

Fill in the blanks with the corresponding Michoacan morphemes:

house	________________	my	________________
dog	________________	your	________________
cornfield	________________	his	________________
		plural	________________

What does [pelomes] mean in this language?

What would be the form for 'my cornfields' in this language? For 'his dogs'?

4. Isleta (a dialect of Southern Tiwa—New Mexico, U.S.A.)

1.	[temiban]	I went	4.	[mimiay]	he was going
2.	[amiban]	you went	5.	[tewanban]	I came
3.	[temiwe]	I am going	6.	[tewanhi]	I will come

List the morphemes corresponding to the following English translations:

I	____________	present progressive	____________
you	____________	past progressive	____________
he	____________	past	____________
go	____________	future	____________
come	____________		

What type of affixes are the subject morphemes?

What type of affixes are the tense morphemes?

What is the order of morphemes in this language?

How would you say the following in this language?

he went ______________________________

I will go ______________________________

you were coming ______________________________

HINT ... The term progressive refers to an ongoing action. In English, the progressive is formed by adding the inflectional affix -ing to a verb and adding the present (am, are, is) or past tense (was, were) of the auxiliary verb 'be'. So, *I am going* is present progressive, and *he was going* is past progressive. Remember, the progressive may not be formed in the same way in Isleta as in English. Remember as well that morphemes can have the same form but different functions!

5. Isthmus Zapoteco (Mexico) Note: [ñ] is a palatal nasal

1.	[ñee]	foot	12.	[kazigidu]	our chins
2.	[kañee]	feet	13.	[zike]	shoulder
3.	[ñeebe]	his foot	14.	[zikebe]	his shoulder
4.	[kañeebe]	his feet	15.	[kazikelu?]	your shoulders
5.	[ñeelu?]	your foot	16.	[diaga]	ear
6.	[kañeetu]	your (pl) feet	17.	[kadiagatu]	your (pl) ears
7.	[kañeedu]	our feet	18.	[kadiagadu]	our ears
8.	[kazigi]	chins	19.	[bisozedu]	our father
9.	[zigibe]	his chin	20.	[bisozetu]	your (pl) father
10.	[zigilu?]	your chin	21.	[kabisozetu]	your (pl) fathers
11.	[kazigitu]	your (pl) chins			

List the morphemes of Isthmus Zapoteco which correspond to each of the following words:

foot	________________	your	________________
shoulder	________________	our	________________
father	________________	his	________________
chin	________________	plural	________________
ear	________________		
your (pl)	________________		

What is the order of morphemes in Isthmus Zapoteco in terms of nouns, possessive determiners and plural?

TWO REMINDERS:

1. An affix is an infix only when it is inserted inside a morpheme.
2. Don't forget to use morphological boundary markers (i.e., dashes) for all bound affixes (prefixes, suffixes, and affixes). Root words do not need boundary markers.

6. Fore (Papua New Guinea)

1. [natuwi]	I ate yesterday	8. [natuni]	We ate yesterday
2. [nagasuwi]	I ate today.	9. [nagasuni]	We ate today.
3. [nakuwi]	I will eat.	10. [nagasusi]	We (dual) ate today.
4. [nata:ni]	You ate yesterday.	11. [nakuni]	We will eat.
5. [nata:naw]	You ate yesterday?	12. [nakusi]	We (dual) will eat.
6. [nakiyi]	He will eat.	13. [nata:wi]	They ate yesterday.
7. [nakiyaw]	He will eat?	14. [nata:si]	They (dual) ate yesterday.

- Don't forget that what are inflectional affixes in many languages can be translated into separate words in English.
- 'yesterday', 'today', and 'tomorrow' are translations of the English past, present, and future tenses (respectively).

Identify the Fore morphemes that correspond to the following English words:

I	________________	eat	________________
he	________________	yesterday	________________
we	________________	today	________________
they	________________	will	________________
we (dual)	________________	question	________________
they (dual)	________________	statement	________________

Describe the order of the morphemes in terms of personal pronouns, question/statement markers, verbs, and adverbs.

Give the Fore words for the following:

He ate yesterday? ________________________________

They (dual) will eat? ________________________________

They ate today. ________________________________

MORPHOPHONEMICS

Morphemes do not always have the same form. Allomorphs are the different forms of a morpheme. Consider the following English example.

⇒ **The Allomorphs …** The English plural morpheme -s has three different phonetic forms:

[-s] in words like 'cats',
[-z] in words like 'dogs', and
[-əz] in words like 'dishes'.

⇒ **The Conditioning Environment …** Which phonetic form is realized depends on the phonological characteristics of the final segment in the preceding word:

[-s] occurs after a base ending in a voiceless consonant that is not strident;
[-z] occurs after a base ending in a voiced consonant that is not strident;
[-əz] occurs after a base ending in a strident consonant.

The specific environment in which the different allomorphs occur is often referred to as the distribution of the allomorphs. This interaction between morphology and phonology is called **morphophonemics**.

For more information on morphophonemics, visit www.pearsoned.ca/ogrady and select Chapter 4, morphophonemics.

Practice! Find the allomorphs in the following data from Luiseño.

<u>**Luiseño (Southern California)**</u>

1.	[nokaamay]	my son	13.	[pokaamay]	his son
2.	[ʔoki]	your house	14.	[poki]	his house
3.	[potaanat]	his blanket	15.	[notaanat]	my blanket
4.	[ʔohuukapi]	your pipe	16.	[pohuukapi]	his pipe
5.	[ʔotaanat]	your blanket	17.	[nohuukapi]	my pipe
6.	[noki]	my house	18.	[ʔokaamay]	your son
7.	[ʔokim]	your houses	19.	[pompeewum]	their wives
8.	[nokaamayum]	my sons	20.	[camhuukapim]	our pipes
9.	[popeew]	his wife	21.	[ʔotaanatum]	your blankets
10.	[ʔopeew]	your wife	22.	[pomkaamay]	their son
11.	[camtaanat]	our blanket	23.	[campeewum]	our wives
12.	[camhuukapi]	our pipe	24.	[pomkim]	their houses

List the Luiseño morphemes that correspond to the following English words:

son	____________	my	____________
house	____________	his	____________
blanket	____________	your	____________
wife	____________	their	____________
pipe	____________	our	____________

What are the two allomorphs of the Luiseño plural marker?

____

State the environment in which each of the allomorphs occurs. Be very general!

a. ____

b. ____

REVIEW! REVIEW! Make sure you know how to:

- define morphological terms
- divide a word into its morphemes
- assign lexical categories
- build word trees
- identify inflection and derivation
- construct compound words
- recognize endocentric and exocentric compounds
- recognize morphological processes used to build words
- do morphological analysis
- identify morphemes and morphological processes in unfamiliar languages
- find allomorphs

QUESTIONS? PROBLEMS? DIFFICULTIES?

CHAPTER 5. SYNTAX: THE ANALYSIS OF SENTENCE STRUCTURE

Syntax is the study of how speakers of a language are able to combine words into sentences in order to convey any and all thoughts. Some of the important topics and concepts found in this chapter include:

1. lexical and non-lexical categories
2. phrases
3. phrase structure and phrase structure tests
4. sentences
5. complement clauses
6. complement options
7. Merge and Move
8. deep and surface structure
9. Yes/No and wh-questions
10. Inversion, Wh-Movement and Do-Insertion
11. Verb raising
12. coordination, modifiers, and passives

WORDS

Words are an important part of a language's grammar. A speaker's lexicon (mental dictionary) contains information on the pronunciation and meaning of individual words. It also contains information on the syntactic category to which a word belongs.

There are two types of syntactic categories: lexical and non-lexical. Some of the major characteristics of each include:

Lexical:
- words that have meaning
- words that can be inflected
- includes nouns (N), verbs (V), adjectives (A), prepositions (P), and adverbs (Adv)

Non-Lexical:
- words whose meaning is harder to define
- words that have a grammatical function
- includes determiners (Det), auxiliary verbs (Aux), conjunctions (Con), and degree words (Deg)

See **Table 5.1** on **pg. 148** of the text for some examples of lexical (content) and non-lexical (function) words.

The lexical category to which a word belongs can be determined by examining (1) its meaning, (2) the type of inflectional affixes that it can take, and (3) the non-lexical category words with which it can co-occur. Words can often belong to more than one category, so you also need to pay close attention to how the word is being used in a sentence.

PRACTICE WITH SYNTACTIC CATEGORIES

Each sentence below has some words underlined in it. Identify the category of each underlined word. Note that the underlined word can be either lexical or non-lexical.

1. Pamela's heart beat really fast and her hands trembled as she listened to the intermittent knocking on the front door of her shanty located near the railroad tracks beside a hobo jungle and she thought, "That's a bum rap, if ever I heard one."

2. The railroad agent told the Navajo, "The coming of the Iron Horse will bring great prosperity to your people."

3. "The leg, he is fractured," he said in broken English.

4. The Great Barrier Reef is 900 miles long and Wilmer Chanti, the great explorer, says it could be circumnavigated in forty days.

5. When I turned the key to open my lab door, I thought that it would be a very dull day, until I noticed that my little cucaracha had flopped over on his back, and was waving his little legs frantically, and I realized that someone had bugged my bug.

6. It was a rather dark, but calm night, its green clarity diluted by my roommates who, as usual, were making cutting remarks as they drank that bottle of old scotch.

7. "I hate pineapples," said Tom dolefully.

8. Here's how to make a fortune. Buy fifty female pigs and fifty male deer. Then you will have a hundred sows and bucks.

Reminder! There are two types of auxiliary verbs: modal and non-modal. Modal auxiliary verbs include *will, would, can, could, may, must, should, might* . . . . Non-modal auxiliary verbs include all the different forms of *be* (*am, are, is, was, were*) and *have* (*has, had*).

Go back over the above exercise, and for any word that you identified as an auxiliary verb, determine if it is a modal or non-modal auxiliary verb.

PHRASES

Words are grouped together to form phrases. There are three important components to a phrase.

⇒ **Heads.** A phrase must have a head. The head of a phrase is the obligatory nucleus around which the phrase is built. Four lexical categories usually function as the head of a phrase, thereby allowing for four types of phrases.

1. **NP** – noun phrase
2. **AP** – adjective phrase
3. **VP** – verb phrase
4. **PP** – prepositional phrase

The head of a noun phrase, of course, is a noun. The head of an adjective phrase, an adjective. The head of a verb phrase, a verb, and the head of a prepositional phrase, a preposition.

⇒ **Specifiers.** A phrase can optionally contain a specifier. Specifiers help to make the meaning of the head more precise. Specifiers mark phrasal boundaries. In English, specifiers occur before the head, thus marking the beginning of a phrase.

1. Determiners – specify a noun
   e.g., the, a, these, that …
2. Adverbs – specify a verb
   e.g., always, often, never …
3. Degree words – specify an adjective or a preposition
   e.g., very, quite, really …

⇒ **Complements.** A phrase can also optionally contain a complement. Complements provide more information about entities that are implied by the head of the phrase. Like specifiers, complements also provide information on the boundary of a phrase. In English, complements come after the head, thus marking the end of a phrase. Complements are typically other phrases.

REMINDER! REMINDER!

Specifiers can help determine the category to which a word belongs. This is because the type of specifier found in a phrase depends on the category of the head. So, if a word can occur with a determiner, it is a noun, if it can occur with an adverb, it is a verb, and if it can occur with a degree word it is an adjective!

⇒ A phrase can consist of a single word or many words. If a phrase consists of a single word, that word must be the head of the phrase. If a phrase consists of many words, the phrase may consist of

- a specifier and a head,
- a head and a complement, or
- a specifier, a head, and a complement.

Below are some examples of these three possibilities for each type of phrase.

1. Noun Phrase (NP)

a. **mud** – contains only the head noun (**mud**)

b. **the mud** – contains a specifier (**the**) and the head noun (**mud**)

c. **mud on the floor** – contains the head noun (**mud**) and a complement prepositional phrase (**on the floor**)

d. **the mud on the floor** – contains a specifier (**the**), the head noun (**mud**), and a complement prepositional phrase (**on the floor**)

The prepositional phrase **on the floor** consists of a head preposition (**on**) and a complement noun phrase (**the floor**). The noun phrase **the floor** then consists of a specifier (**the**) and a head noun (**floor**).

2. Adjective Phrase (AP)

a. **happy** – contains only the head adjective (**happy**)

b. **very happy** – contains a specifier (**very**) and the head adjective (**happy**)

c. **happy with the results** – contains the head adjective (**happy**) and a complement prepositional phrase (**with the results**)

d. **very happy with the results** – contains a specifier (**very**), the head adjective (**happy**), and a complement prepositional phrase (**with the results**)

The prepositional phrase **with the results** consists of a head preposition (**with**) and a complement noun phrase (**the results**). The noun phrase **the results** then consists of a specifier (**the**) and a head noun (**results**).

3. Verb Phrase (VP)

a. **sings** – contains only the head verb (**sing**)

b. **often sings** – contains a specifier (**often**) and the head verb (**sings**)

c. **sings a song** – contains the head verb (**sing**) and a complement noun phrase (**a song**)

d. **often sings a song** – contains a specifier (**often**), the head verb (**sings**), and a a complement noun phrase (**a song**)

The complement noun phrase **a song** consists of a specifier (**a**) and a head noun (**song**).

4. Prepositional Phrase (PP)

a. **in the car** – contains the head preposition (**in**) and a complement noun phrase (**the car**)

b. **almost in the car** – contains a specifier (**almost**), the head preposition (**in**) and a complement noun phrase (**the car**)

The complement noun phrase **the car** contains a specifier (**the**) and a head noun (**car**).

Now ... Think of an example of

⇒ A noun phrase containing a specifier, a head noun, and a complement.
⇒ An adjective phrase containing a specifier and a head adjective.
⇒ A verb phrase containing a head verb and a complement.
⇒ A prepositional phrase containing a head preposition and a complement.

REMINDER! REMINDER!

Prepositional phrases are different from the other three types of phrase in that prepositional phrases must always contain a complement, and this complement is a noun phrase.

Practice ...

For each of the following phrases, determine the head of the phrase, the specifier, and the complement. Remember that every phrase must have a head but that specifiers and complements are optional! The first is done for you.

	SPECIFIER	HEAD	COMPLEMENT
the rat	the	rat	none
men	______	______	______
in the barn	______	______	______
really mean	______	______	______
worked	______	______	______
worked at the station	______	______	______
extremely boring	______	______	______
that house on the corner	______	______	______
never walks to the park	______	______	______
very small	______	______	______
in the room	______	______	______
awfully cute	______	______	______
seldom smiles	______	______	______
swept the floor	______	______	______
the poem about love	______	______	______
pancakes	______	______	______

Now ... Go back and determine the type of each phrase. Remember: the lexical category of the head determines the type of phrase. If you're having trouble identifying the lexical category of the head, refer back to the Reminder box on pg. 107 of this guide.

PHRASE STRUCTURE TESTS

There are a number of tests that can be done to determine whether a group of words is or is not a phrase. Three frequently used tests are the Substitution Test, the Movement Test, and the Coordination Test. Be careful though: not every test works for every phrase.

Substitution Test

The Substitution Test states that a group of words is a phrase if you can substitute words such as 'they', 'there', or 'do so', and still be grammatical. The word used as a substitute also tells you the type of phrase you have.

NP: A noun phrase can be substituted with a pronoun

e.g., **The boys** played in the mud. **They** played in the mud.
(they = the boys)

VP: A verb phrase can be substituted with 'do so'

e.g., The girls will **play in the mud**, if the boys **do so.**
(do so = play in the mud)

PP: A prepositional phrase can be substituted with 'there'

e.g., The boys played **in the mud**. The boys played **there**.
(there = in the mud)

Movement Test

The Movement Test states that a group of words is a phrase if it can be moved to another position in the sentence and still be grammatical.

e.g., The children bought candy **at the store**. ⟶
At the store, the children bought candy.

Coordination Test

According to this test, a group of words is a phrase if it can be joined to another group of words using a conjunction (*and, but, or*) and still be grammatical.

e.g., The children **bought candy** and **left the store**.
– two verb phrases joined with the conjunction *and*

Try this ...

1. Apply the substitution test to determine which of the bracketed sequences of words in the following sentences are phrases.

    1. [Juanita and Juan] arrived [in San Juan] [on Epiphany].
    2. The cabbage [rolls were] salty.
    3. They moved [the desk with the wooden top].
    4. Little Andrew swallowed [all the pills].
    5. The polar bears [were swimming across] the lake.
    6. Brendan is [writing a ballad about Canadian soldiers in Cyprus].

2. Apply the movement test to determine which of the bracketed sequences in the following sentences are phrases.

    1. The [army was surrounded] by the enemy.
    2. Leona likes [Viennese waltzes and Argentinean tangos].
    3. Jean ate his lunch [in the revolving restaurant].
    4. Eat, drink, and [be merry for] today will become yesterday.

3. Use a conjunction (and, but, or) and join each of the following phrases with a phrase of the same type. You might want to first use the substitution test to determine the type of phrase!

    1. the new desk
    2. assembled the new desk
    3. new
    4. in a hole
    5. rather huge
    6. worked on a movie
    7. beside the fence
    8. really lovely
    9. talked to the girls
    10. a dentist

PHRASE STRUCTURE TREES

Specifiers, heads, and complements are arranged using the X' (X-bar) schema, in which X stands for any head.

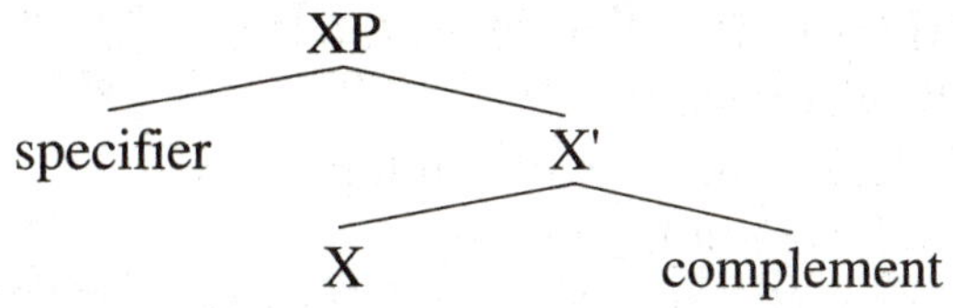

The representation of a phrase using the above schema is often referred to as a tree diagram.

⇒ Some things to remember about tree diagrams:

- All tree diagrams will have an XP, X', and X.
- All phrases have a head (X).
- If there is a specifier, it is attached at the XP level
- If there is a complement, it is attached at the X' level.

The above applies to all phrases (NP, VP, AP, and PP).

⇒ See **Figures 5.2, 5.3, 5.4, 5.5**, and **5.6** on **pgs. 152, 153** and **154** of the text for examples of tree diagrams of phrases containing only heads, specifiers and heads, specifiers, heads and complements, and heads and complements.

Exercise! Draw tree diagrams for each of the following phrases. Remember: specifiers come before the head, and complements after the head.

1. the rat
2. men
3. in the barn
4. really mean
5. ran
6. ran into the shed
7. rather boring
8. hate those pancakes
9. the house on the corner
10. very small
11. in the room
12. awfully cute
13. seldom smiles
14. swept the floor
15. fond of candy
16. silly
17. the poem about love
18. read the poem
19. jumped over the barn
20. usually eats lunch

QUICK REMINDER:

Use the Substitution Test to help you determine the type of phrase you are dealing with. Remember: the Substitution Test not only tells you if a group of words is or is not a phrase; it can also tell you the type of phrase you have. Refer back to pgs. 111 and 112 for more information.

SENTENCES

A sentence is the largest unit of syntactic analysis. Sentences have the same structure as do phrases in that they consist of a specifier, head, and complement.

⇒ **NP.** This noun phrase is typically referred to as the subject. See **Figures 5.2a, 5.3a**, and **5.5a** on **pgs. 153** and **154** of the text for some examples of diagrammed NPs. The subject is the specifier of I.

⇒ **I. (Infl)** This is the obligatory head of the sentence, and is used to refer to inflection. There are two possibilities for I: +pst (past) and –pst (non-past), +pst is used for sentences in the past tense, and –pst is used for sentences in either the present or future tense.

Modal auxiliaries occur under I. This is because modals have an inherent tense (non-past) and so I is a natural place for them to occur. I, then, has two possibilities:

- inflection alone (either +pst or –pst),
- inflection (–pst) and a modal auxiliary.

⇒ **VP.** This verb phrase is typically referred to as the predicate. The VP is the complement of I. See **Figures 5.2b, 5.3b, 5.4** and **5.6a** on **pgs. 153** and **154** of the text for some examples of diagrammed VPs.

Sentences, like phrases, are built according to the X' schema. Since I is the head of a sentence, IP is used to represent this syntactic unit.

Below are two examples of fully diagrammed sentences: the first without a modal auxiliary, and the second with a modal auxiliary. For another example of each possibility, see **Figures 5.8** and **5.9** on **pg. 156** of the text.

(1) *The children read a book.*

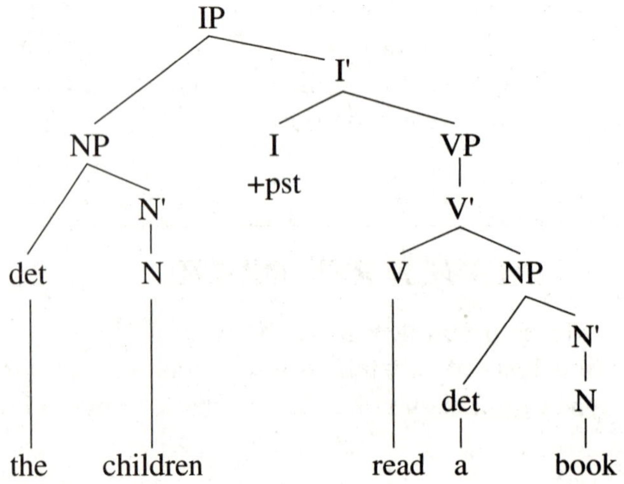

(2) *The children might read a book.*

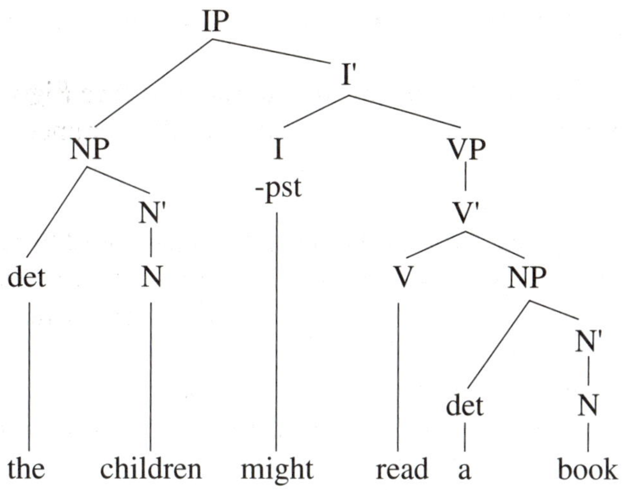

Practice! Draw a tree diagram for each of the following sentences.

1. A penguin walked into the room.
2. Carl might sell that car.
3. Dogs should always go for a walk.
4. Abner concealed the document.
5. Those monsters never hide under the bed.
6. The air smells really fresh.
7. The children played with a dinosaur.
8. George seems tired of studying.
9. Grandparents may live in condominiums.
10. Marge usually watches the sunset.

QUICK REMINDER

A noun phrase (NP), a prepositional phrase (PP), or an adjective phrase (AP) are all potential complements of a verb. The particular complement that occurs depends on the verb. Some verbs can take more than one complement!

COMPLEMENT CLAUSES

In addition to noun phrases, adjective phrases, and prepositional phrases, a sentence (IP) may also function as a complement. When a sentence functions as a complement, it can occur in the complement position of a verb phrase. The sentence contained within the verb phrase is called a complement clause (CP). The sentence within which the CP is found is called the matrix clause.

A CP is like any other type of phrase in that it consists of a specifier, a head, and a complement.

⇒ **Specifier.** The specifier position of a CP functions as a landing site for phrases undergoing the Move operation (see the section on Move).

⇒ **Complementizer.** The head of a CP is a complementizer (C). Complementizers include words such as *that*, *if*, and *whether*.

⇒ **IP.** The complement of a complementizer is an IP (i.e., a sentence).

Below is a tree diagram of the sentence *John thinks that Mary will win*, which contains a CP inside the VP. See **Figures 5.11** and **5.12** on **pg. 161** of the text for another example. See **Table 5.9** on **pg. 162** of the text for examples of verbs that can have CP complements.

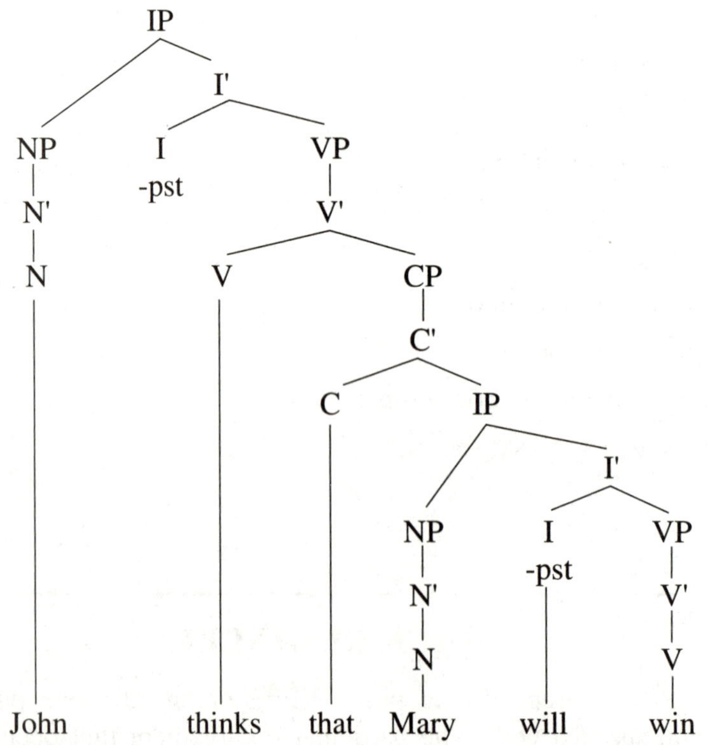

Practice! Practice! Draw a tree diagram for each of the following sentences.

1. Stan hopes that Sean will become a pilot.
2. Nancy believes that aliens exist.
3. Sailors know that they could drown at sea.
4. The realtor wondered whether Louise sold the house.
5. The passengers thought that the plane would never land.

SOME HINTS FOR DRAWING PHRASE STRUCTURE TREES

1. Every sentence (IP) has the following structure.

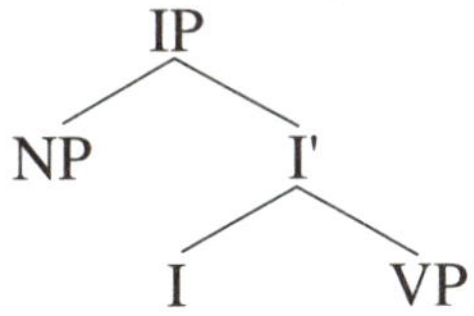

2. Every sentence contains I. Identify the tense of the sentence. +pst is used if a sentence is in the past tense, and –pst if the sentence is in either the present or future tense. If the sentence contains a modal auxiliary, this auxiliary occurs under I and I will be –pst.

3. Every sentence has a verb. Identify the verb. Check if this verb has a specifier and/or a complement. Remember that the specifier of a verb is an adverb and marks the beginning of the phrase. If there is a complement, it can be either a phrase or a sentence.

   - If the complement is a phrase, identify the type of phrase and then diagram the phrase using the X' schema.
   - If the complement is a sentence, it will begin with the following structure.

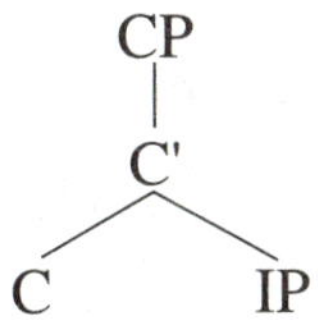

   Identify the complementizer. Since a CP contains an IP, you will also need to identify and diagram the NP, I, and VP for this embedded IP.

4. Every sentence has a subject NP. Identify the noun. Check if this noun has a specifier and/or a complement. Remember that the specifier of a noun is a determiner and that this determiner marks the beginning of this noun phrase. If there is a complement, it will be a prepositional phrase. Diagram this phrase using the X' schema.

For more hints on drawing tree diagrams of phrases and sentences, see the **Appendix** to Chapter Five on **pgs. 181–183** of the text.

MORE SENTENCES

The following exercise contains many examples of sentences with and without complement clauses. Draw a tree diagram for each. Watch out: they get harder!

1. The repairman fixed the watch.
2. Neighbors can be unfriendly.
3. Nurses never complain.
4. The train often leaves on time.
5. The castle fell into the sea.
6. Those men on the shore saw a signal.
7. The rabbit sometimes hides under the bridge.
8. The secretary should mail the proposal.
9. Children are very curious.
10. Flowers usually bloom in the summer.
11. That soup tastes really great.
12. The rabbit might eat the lilies.
13. Sally lives in a house by the sea.
14. The driver of that car sped down the highway.
15. The media reported that the candidate won the election.
16. The salesman wondered if those customers would buy the car.
17. George hoped that Fred would win the car.
18. Kayleigh usually thinks that playing in the park is fun.
19. The smugglers suspected that the police might arrive.
20. The captain hoped that the tourists would perhaps see a whale.

MERGE

Merge is an operation contained within the computational system of the grammar. Merge is responsible for building the phrase structure in a manner compatible with the X' schema. Essentially, Merge combines words together to make phrases, phrases to make sentences and sentences to make larger sentences.

⇒ The following example illustrates how Merge operates.

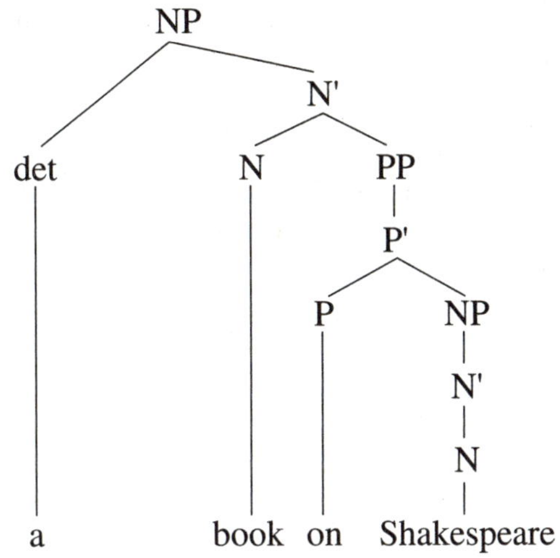

Merge created the above complex phrase by combining the noun phrase "Shakespeare" with the preposition "on" to create the prepositional phrase "on Shakespeare". This phrase was then combined with the noun "book" and the specifier "a" to create the noun phrase "a book on Shakespeare". Merge continues to operate in this way to create entire sentences.

Complement Options

In addition to using the X' schema, Merge must combine words into phrases and sentences in a manner consistent with the complement options of the individual words. Essentially, individual words in a sentence must occur with complements of the right type for the sentence to be grammatical. The complement(s) with which a word can occur are called its complement options.

⇒ **Think...** Does the verb *throw* require a complement or can it occur without a complement? If it requires a complement, what type of complement is needed? If it occurs without this complement or with a complement of a different type, is the resulting sentence grammatical or ungrammatical? What about the verb *become*? What type of complement does it require? What about the verb *arrive*? Does it require a complement?

See **Table 5.5** on **pg. 158** of the text for some examples of different verb complements in English. See **Tables 5.6, 5.7,** and **5.8** on **pgs. 159** and **160** of the text for some examples of complement options for nouns, adjectives, and prepositions.

Information on the complement options of words, along with the meaning and pronunciation of words, is found in a speaker's lexicon. Information about a word's complement options is often referred to as subcategorization.

Try This! Determine the complement options that the verbs listed below require. Do this by thinking of grammatical and ungrammatical sentences containing the verb.

- panic
- watch
- imagine
- write
- wonder
- play

Nouns, adjectives and prepositions also have restrictions on the types of complements with which they can and cannot occur. Determine the complement options which the following words require. Start by identifying the lexical category of the word and then think of grammatical and ungrammatical sentences containing the word.

- pleasure
- with
- contribution
- intelligent
- at
- upset

MOVE

Move is a second syntactic operation. Move transports elements from one position in a sentence to another. This is all that a Move operation can do: Move cannot change the categories of words, nor can it eliminate any part of the structure.

There are three important points to remember about how Move operates.

⇒ **CP.** Move transports elements to positions with a CP. For this to occur, every IP must be found within a larger CP. This CP is a shell that contains an IP.

- Remember that a CP can function as a complement clause, in which case it is embedded in a larger sentence. When a CP is embedded within a larger sentence, C can contain a complementizer such as *that*, *if*, or *whether*. Refer back to **Figure 5.12** on **pg. 161** of the text for an example of a sentence with an embedded CP.

- For CP shells containing an IP (i.e., all other CPs), C contains information on whether the sentence is a question or a statement: if C contains +Q, the structure is a question, and if C is empty, it is a statement. It is the +Q which can trigger a Move operation. See **Figure 5.14** on **pg. 163** of the text for an example of an IP within a CP shell.

⇒ **Trace.** Moved elements leave behind a trace (t). A trace records (1) that a movement occurred and (2) where in the structure the moved element originated. This is necessary as Move cannot change the structure that Merge builds.

⇒ **Levels of Representation.** Two levels of representation result: deep and surface structure.

- Merge occurs first to build the syntactic structure. The structure that Merge generates is called the deep structure (D-structure).

- Move may then apply. The surface structure (S-structure) is the result of applying any additional operations, such as Move. The surface structure is often called the final syntactic form.

If a Move operation has taken place, then the deep and surface structure are usually not the same. If no Move operation takes place, then the deep and surface structures are the same.

QUESTIONS

Merge is responsible for building the structure of a sentence using both subcategorization information and the X' schema. However, Merge cannot create all the structures of a language. Some structures require a second operation. Move transforms an existing structure (e.g., a statement) into another type of structure (e.g., a question) by transporting elements from one position in a sentence to another.

Move operates to create both yes-no and wh-questions.

Yes-no Questions

⇒ Yes-no questions are so named because the response to such a question is usually 'yes' or 'no'. Yes-no questions are formed by moving an auxiliary verb from its position in I to the complementizer position within a CP. This is informally called Inversion.

Inversion: Move I to C
e.g., Mary **will** leave → **Will** Mary **t** leave

After Merge:

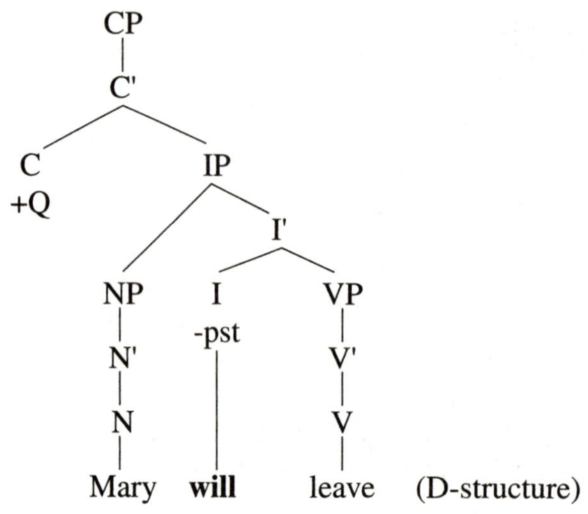

After Inversion:

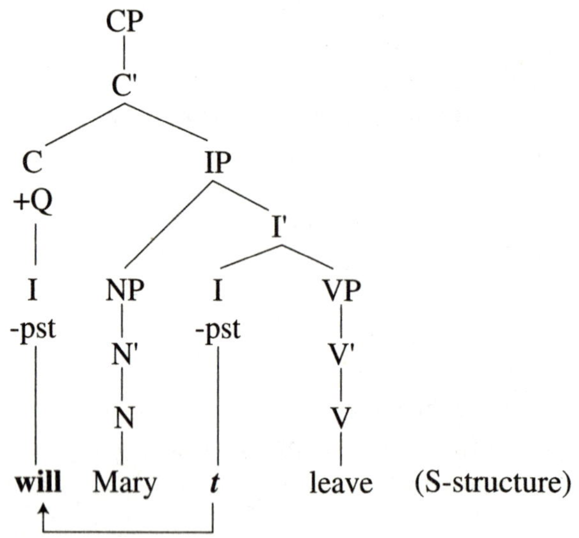

⇒ Many sentences do not contain an auxiliary verb. Yet these sentences can still be changed into a yes-no question. This is done by inserting the auxiliary verb *do* into the sentence. This is called Do-Insertion and is an example of an operation that adds elements to a tree structure.

Do-Insertion: Insert "do" into an empty I position.

eg., Mary left → Mary **did** leave → **Did** Mary **t** leave

After Merge:

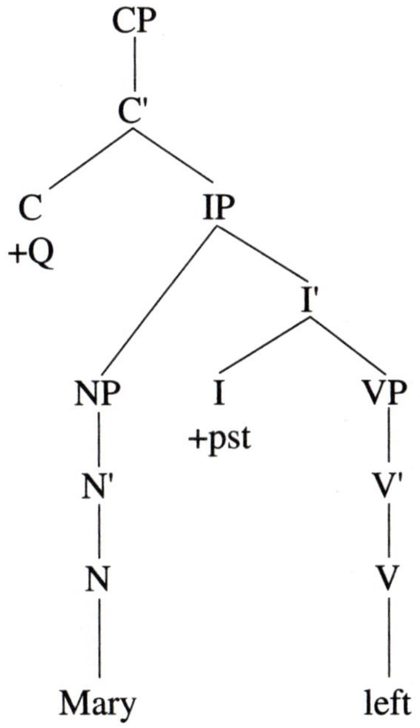

(D-structure)

After Do-Insertion:

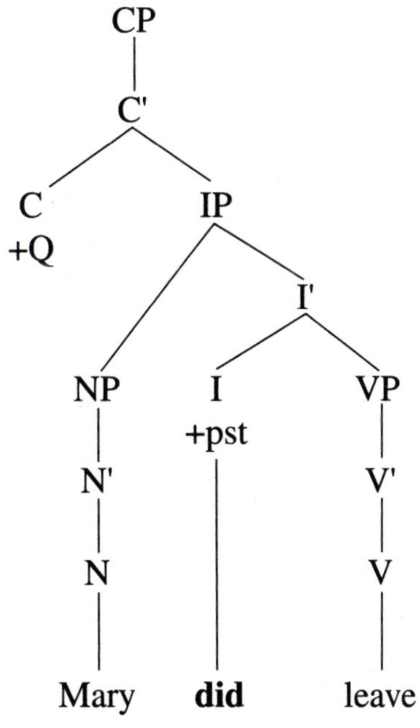

After Inversion:

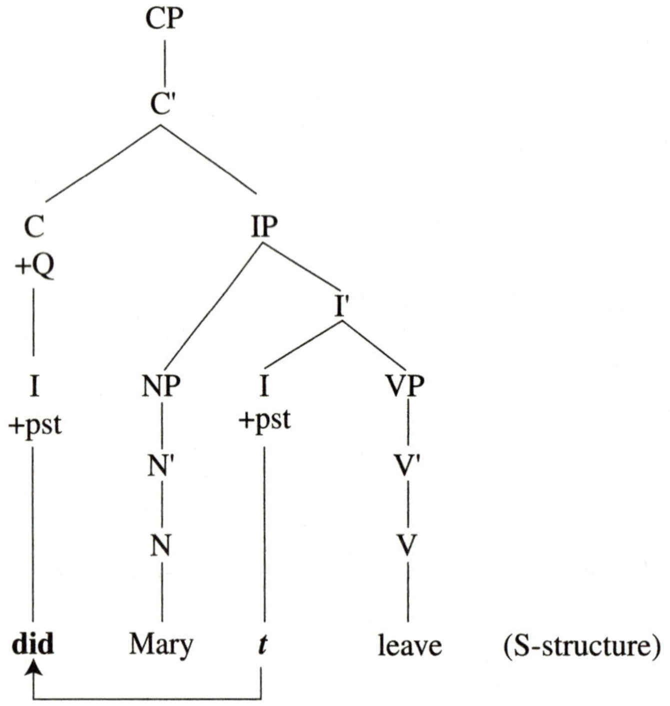

Wh-Questions

⇒ Wh-Questions are so named because they begin with a wh-word. *who*, *what*, and *which* are all examples of wh-words. *who* and *what* are analyzed as nouns; *which* is a determiner. Wh-questions are the result of Wh-Movement. Wh-Movement is normally followed by Inversion.

Wh-Movement: Move a wh-phrase to the specifier position under CP.

e.g., George **should** buy *what* → *What* **should** George **t** buy *t*

After Merge:

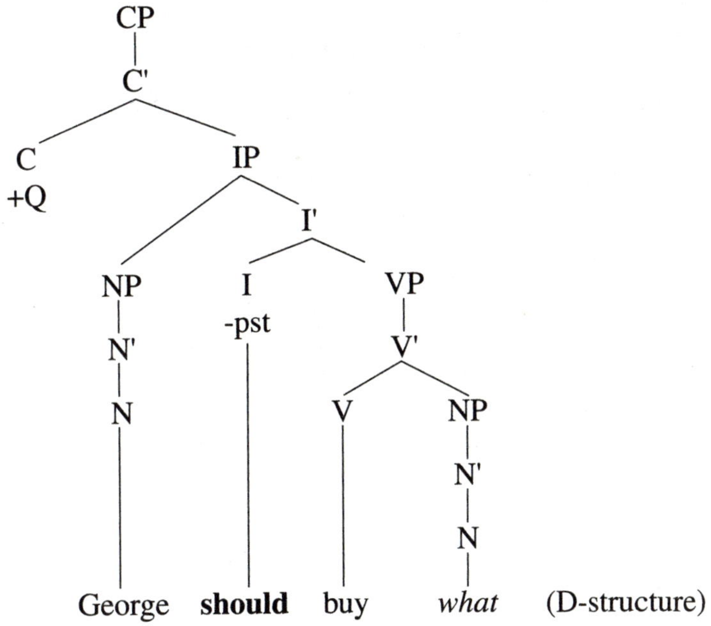

After Wh-Movement and Inversion:

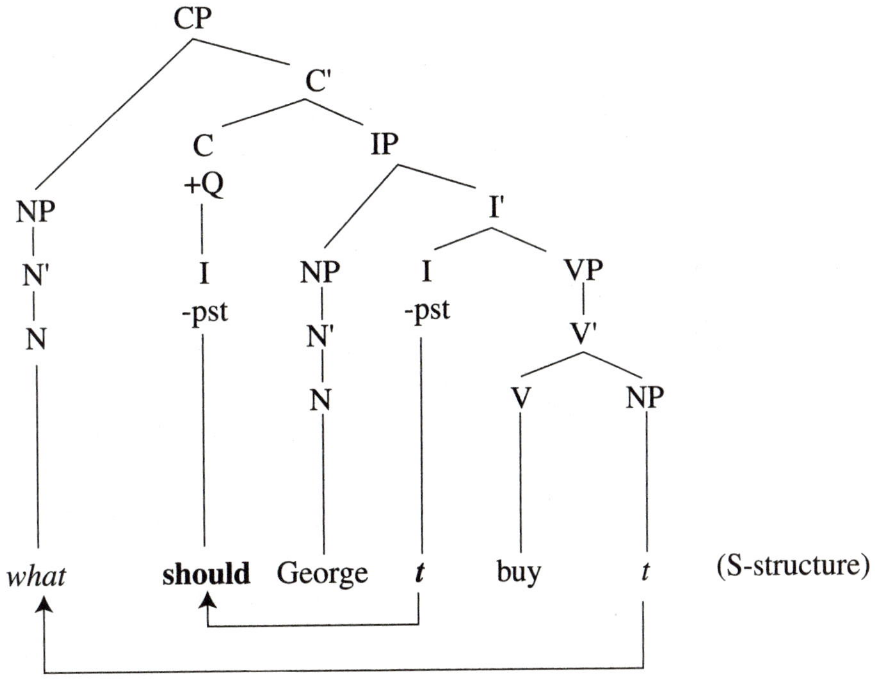

Think! Do-Insertion can also occur during the formation of wh-questions.

e.g., George bought *what*. → *What* George bought *t* →

What George **did** buy *t* → *What* **did** George **t** buy *t*

Try drawing a tree diagram of both the deep structure and surface structure for the above sentence. You do not need to draw any intermediate structures. Indicate with arrows all of the movements. Do this on the surface structure.

⇒ Wh-Movement can move a wh-phrase occurring as the complement of the verb (as in the previous example) or it can move a wh-phrase occurring in the subject position.

e.g., *Who* broke the lamp → *Who t* broke the lamp

After Merge:

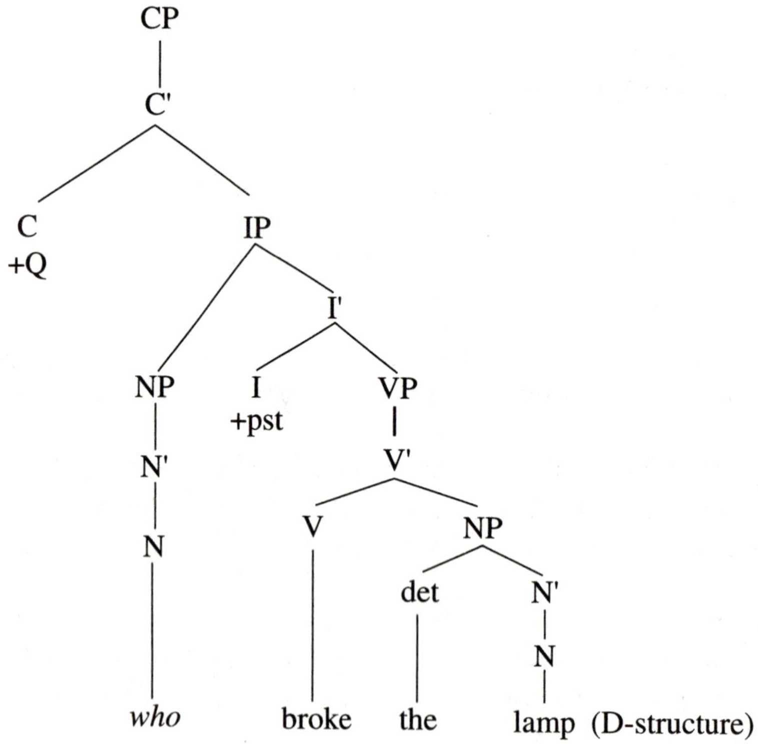

After Wh-Movement:

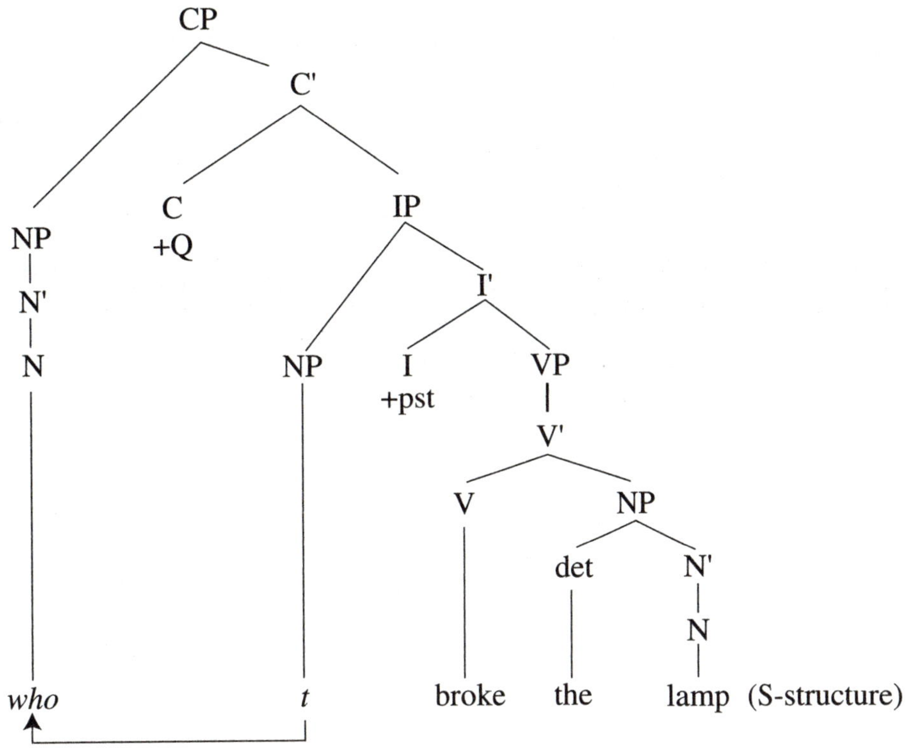

Think... Compare the above deep and surface structures. Is the word order in the deep and surface structure the same? Is Do-Insertion required when Wh-movement moves a subject NP?

See **Figures 5.15, 5.17, 5.18, 5.19, 5.20** and **5.21** on **pgs. 164, 167, 168, 170**, and **171** of the text for more examples of tree diagrams of the deep and surface structures of sentences in which Inversion, Do-Insertion, and Wh-Movement take place.

Try This! For each of the following sentences, draw a tree diagram for both the deep and surface structures. On the surface structure, indicate with arrows the elements that have moved and where they have moved.

1. Will Paul enjoy the trip?
2. Which coat should Joan wear?
3. What did the spy uncover?
4. Who can see the shore?
5. Do beagles always bark?

Remember...	1. To include a trace for each movement. 2. That Wh-movement moves an entire phrase, called a wh-phrase.

VERB RAISING

Move can also transport a verb to a new position in the sentence. This is often called Verb Raising. Verb Raising is found in many different languages and can affect auxiliary verbs.

⇒ There are two types of auxiliaries: modal and non-modal. Modal auxiliaries occur in I. Non-modal auxiliaries (*have* and *be*) are a special type of verb. As such, they occur in V. They also take a verb phrase as a complement. Below is an example of a tree diagram for the sentence *The children are reading a book.*

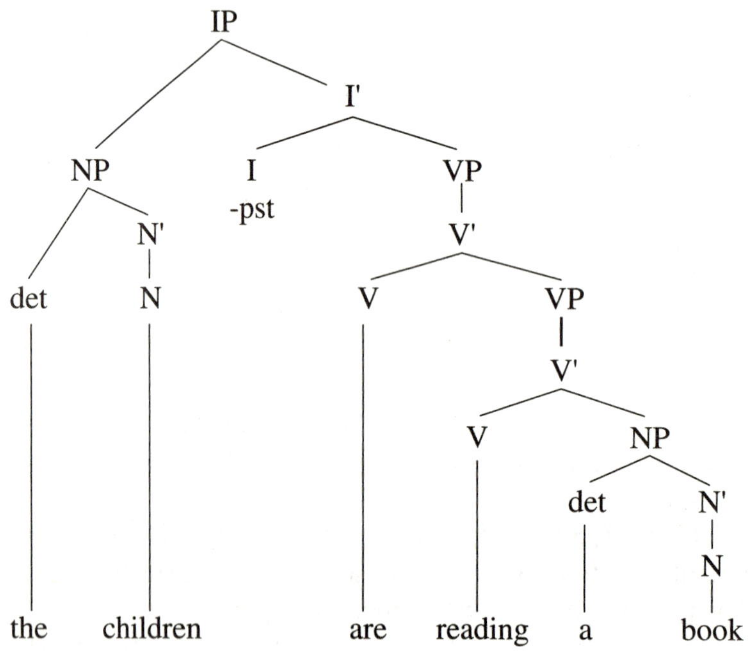

Think... A sentence can have more than one auxiliary. For example, the sentence *The children have been reading a book* contains two non-modal auxiliaries. How would you diagram the verb phrase of this sentence? What about the sentence *The children will be reading a book*, which contains both a modal and a non-modal auxiliary? How would you diagram the verb phrase for this sentence?

⇒ Both modal and non-modal auxiliaries can be inverted to create a yes-no question. Remember that Inversion moves I to C. This is sufficient for modal auxiliaries, as they occur in I. However, since non-modal auxiliaries occur in V, they must be moved from V to I before moving to C. The move from V to I is Verb Raising. (See **Figure 5.25** on **pg. 175** of the text for another example of V to I movement.)

Verb Raising: Move V to I

e.g., Mary **is** leaving → Mary **is t** leaving

After Merge:

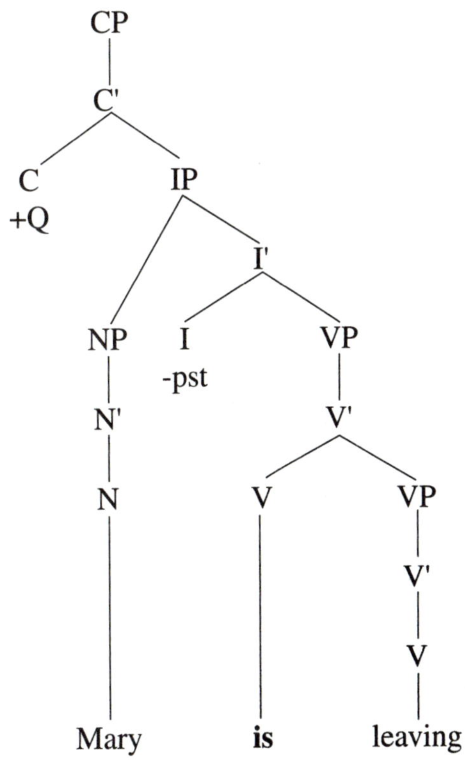

(D-structure)

After Verb Raising:

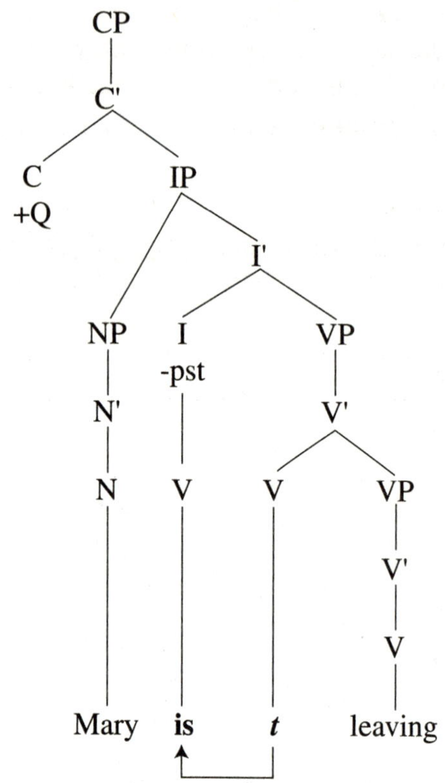

After Inversion:

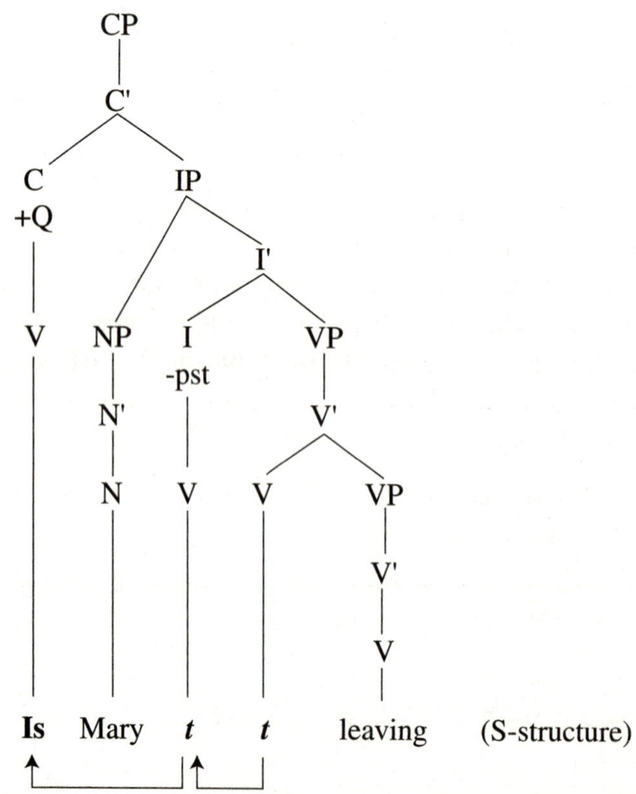

Think! Verb raising can also occur during the formation of wh-questions.

eg., Sylvia **was** thinking *what.* → *What* Sylvia **was** thinking *t* →

What Sylvia **was t** thinking *t* → *What* **was** Sylvia **t t** thinking *t*

Does moving an auxiliary verb from V to I change the word order of the sentence? Does Verb Raising take place if Wh-movement moves a subject NP? Why or why not? Think about Do-Insertion. If this takes place, is Verb Raising needed? Why or why not?

Try drawing a tree diagram of both the deep structure and surface structure for the above sentence. You do not need to draw trees for any intermediate structures. Indicate with arrows all of the movements. Do this on the surface structure.

Try This! For each of the following sentences, draw a tree diagram of both the deep and surface structures.

1. Are the neighbours moving to Dogpound?
2. Which restaurant is closing?
3. Have the elves swept the floor?
4. What was Sally painting?

REMINDER! REMINDER!

Verb Raising is a good example of the variation that occurs across languages. In English only auxiliary (non-modal) verbs can move to I; regular (main) verbs cannot move. What this means is that only auxiliary verbs (both modal and non-modal) can be inverted to create questions. This is not true of all languages. For example, in French, any type of verb can move into I. This means that both regular (main) verbs and auxiliary verbs can be inverted in French. The idea is that all languages use the Move operation, but how this operation is instantiated can vary from language to language!

See **Figures 5.22** and **5.23** on **pgs. 173** and **174** of the text for tree diagrams illustrating Verb Raising in French.

Some Hints…

You need to be able to determine the deep structure for any sentence you are given, and to do so you need to be able to identify any of the movements that have occurred. Remember, Inversion, Wh-movement, and Verb Raising are all applications of the Move operation. Do-Insertion is also a syntactic operation. You may also have to construct a tree diagram of the deep and surface structures.

Here are some clues to help you identify which movements have occurred, and to put surface structure sentences back into their deep structure:

YOU SEE:	YOU THINK:	YOU DO:
A modal auxiliary verb ahead of the subject.	Inversion has taken place.	Put the modal auxiliary back into its deep structure position (I).
A non-modal auxiliary verb ahead of the subject.	Inversion has taken place. Verb Raising has taken place.	Put the non-modal auxiliary back into its deep structure position (V).
A wh-word or phrase.	Wh-Movement has taken place.	Examine each verb in the sentence. Determine if a verb is missing either a subject or an object. Put the wh-word or phrase into that position.
"Do", "Did", or "Does" at the beginning of a sentence, or after a wh-word or phrase.	Do-Insertion has taken place.	Remove "do", "did", or "does" from the sentence.

See the **Appendix** to Chapter 5 on **pgs. 183–185** of the text for more hints on how to analyze sentences involving the Move operation.

TRANSFORMATION WORKSHEET

Draw a tree diagram of both the deep and surface structure for each of the following sentences. Identify any movements that have occurred to derive the surface structure. Be careful: some sentences are already in deep structure!

1. Can the clown amuse that boy?
2. Who does the jury blame?
3. Margo dreamt that Frances was flying to England.
4. Did Bill sell that house?
5. Christopher had been drawing a picture.
6. Has the player left the team?
7. What was Joanne eating?
8. Could the vandals have destroyed those billboards?
9. Colin thinks that girls never phone George.
10. Who might these clothes fit?
11. Does Henry think that Harry will survive in the jungle?
12. Who should be preparing the meal?
13. Were the maids cleaning the house?
14. The jury believed that the prisoner was guilty.
15. Would the winner claim the prize?
16. Dianne knew that Tom might enjoy the meal.
17. What does Mary want?
18. Do children like cake?

TWO IMPORTANT REMINDERS:

1. You are trying to determine which elements have already been moved; therefore, you must **never** move any additional words or phrases!
2. No movements may have occurred, only one movement may have occurred, or more than one movement may have occurred. To find the deep structure, you need to (1) find all instances of Move, and (2) determine if Do-insertion has occurred.

OTHER SYNTACTIC PHENOMENA

Some other syntactic structures include coordinate structures, modifiers, and passives. Each of these structures builds on the basic syntactic system (i.e., Merge and Move) for forming sentences.

Coordination

Coordination joins structures together using a conjunction such as *and*, *but*, or *or*. Some important things to keep in mind:

⇒ Any level of structure (X, X', or XP) can be joined.

⇒ Only structures of the same type can be joined together. That is, a NP must be conjoined with another NP. If structures of different types are joined, the result is an ungrammatical structure.

⇒ Conjoining structures results in a larger structure of the same type. So, joining two NPs together results in a larger NP.

e.g.,	Vs:	[draw]$_{V}$ and [color]$_{V}$ those pictures
	N's:	that [car]$_{N'}$ and [truck]$_{N'}$
	PPs:	[up the stairs]$_{PP}$ and [into the hallway]$_{PP}$

See **Figure 5.26** on **pg. 177** of the text for some examples of tree diagrams of coordinate structures.

Modifiers

Modifiers are words and phrases that denote properties of heads. There are two main types of modifiers.

⇒ Adjective phrases modify nouns, in that they indicate a property of the noun.

e.g., A **very cold** wind is blowing.

⇒ Adverb phrases modify verbs, in that they can provide information on the manner (for example) of the verb.

e.g., The ballerina danced **gracefully**.

Modifiers attach at the XP level. See **Figure 5.28** on **pg. 178** of the text for some examples of diagrams of phrases containing modifiers.

Passives

A sentence may be either active or passive. Active and passive sentences differ in the following ways:

⇒ In an active sentence, the agent (doer of the action) occurs in the subject position. In a passive sentence, this agent is often absent. If the agent is present, it is found within a prepositional phrase that occurs at or near the end of the sentence.

⇒ In a passive sentence, the direct object of the corresponding active sentence usually functions as the subject of the sentence. Verbs that cannot occur with a direct object in an active sentence can also not occur in passive sentences.

e.g., **Active:** The chef prepared the meal.

Passive: The meal was prepared. / The meal was prepared by the chef.

⇒ Passive sentences are formed using NP Movement, another type of Move. NP Movement transports an object from its deep structure position as a complement of the verb to an empty subject position.

e.g., **D-structure:** was prepared the meal

S-structure: *the meal* was prepared *t*

See **Figure 5.30** on **pg. 179** of the text for an example of a tree diagram of the D-structure of a passive sentence. See **Figure 5.31** on **pg. 180** of the text for an example of a tree diagram of the S-structure of a passive sentence.

Exercise! The following exercises will give you some practice with identifying co-ordinate structures, modifiers, and passives.

1. For each of the following coordinate structures, determine the category of the structures that have been joined together.

   a. Stephen watched television but Gloria listened to the radio.
   b. Terry drove the Ninja-Turtle and the Monster-Mutt.
   c. Bill believes that the world is round and that the sun is hot.
   d. Andrea usually eats dinner and goes to bed.

2. Each of the following sentences contains at least one modifier. Identify all the modifiers. For each modifier determine if it is modifying a noun or a verb. Identify the noun or verb that is being modified.

   a. The musicians often play music loudly.
   b. The really awful movie won top prize.
   c. The undercover police-car drove away speedily.

3. Decide if each of the following sentences is active or passive. Remember: a passive sentence does not necessarily include an agent.

   a. That lamp could be fixed.
   b. Those tigers were trained by a professional.
   c. The company should make a donation.
   d. The winner was given a prize.

For each passive sentence, draw a tree diagram of the deep and surface structures. Indicate with arrows on the surface structure the Move that occurred to create the deep structure.

REVIEW REVIEW!! If you can do the following, then you've conquered syntax:

- describe the differences between lexical and non-lexical categories
- assign words to their syntactic category
- determine if a group of words is or is not a phrase
- identify and diagram phrases
- diagram sentences, including those with complement clauses
- determine complement options
- understand the Merge and Move operations
- spot yes-no and wh-questions
- spot Inversion, Wh-movement, Verb Raising, and Do-Insertion
- find the deep structure of a sentence
- recognize coordinate structures, modifiers, and passives

QUESTIONS? PROBLEMS? DIFFICULTIES?

CHAPTER 6. SEMANTICS: THE ANALYSIS OF MEANING

Semantics is the study of meaning in human language. Meaning refers, very generally, to the content of an utterance.

Important concepts and topics in this chapter include:

1. semantic relations
2. theories of meaning
3. concepts
4. lexicalization
5. grammaticalization
6. lexical and structural ambiguity
7. thematic roles
8. pronoun interpretation
9. pragmatics
10. conversation

SEMANTIC RELATIONS

Determining the semantic relations that exist between words, phrases, and sentences constitutes one of the basic notions used in evaluating meaning.

Relations between words:

⇒ **Between words**

- Synonymy. Words which have similar meanings.
- Antonymy. Words which have opposite meanings.
- Polysemy. One word with two or more related meanings.
- Homophony. Two words with the same pronunciation, but different meanings.

See **Tables 6.1, 6.2, 6.3,** and **6.4** on **pgs. 191** and **192** of the text for some English examples of the above relations.

Think.... Polysemy and homophony can result in lexical ambiguity—a single form that has two or more meanings. Think of some examples. Keep in mind ...

- Different words with the same spelling are called homographs.
- Homophones may or may not have the same spelling.
- Homographs, therefore, may or may not be homophones.

Relations between sentences:

⇒ **Between sentences**

- Paraphrase. Two sentences that have very similar meanings.
  e.g., The cat ate the mouse.
  The mouse was eaten by the cat.
- Entailment. Two sentences in which the truth of the first implies the truth of the second, but the truth of the second does not necessarily imply the truth of the first.
  e.g., George killed the burglar.
  The burglar is dead.
- Contradiction. Two sentences such that if one is true, then the second must be false.
  e.g., George is rich.
  George lives in a shelter.

Try this! For each of the following, identify the relation that exists between either the words or the sentences. The first is done for you!

1. test
   exam ___synonyms___
2. Mary sang a solo.
   A solo was sung by Mary. ______________________
3. bug (insect)
   bug (microphone) ______________________
4. Sam is a widower.
   Sam's wife is alive. ______________________
5. The bear attacked a camper.
   The camper is injured. ______________________
6. parent
   offspring ______________________
7. George gave Sally the book.
   George gave the book to Sally. ______________________
8. Nancy brought salmon for dinner.
   There is nothing to eat for dinner. ______________________
9. hungry
   famished ______________________
10. steak (a piece of meat)
    stake (a sharp piece of wood) ______________________

THEORIES OF MEANING

As native speakers of a language, we all know the meaning of a great many words in our language. And if we come across a word whose meaning is unknown to us, we can always look it up in a dictionary! But, to understand the dictionary definition, we need to understand the meanings of the words making up the definition. It is actually difficult to determine the precise meaning of a word; it is easier to determine the semantic relations between words. Think... Without using a dictionary, what is the meaning of the words *spring, bridge,* and *Hawaii*? Some of the theories of meaning outlined below might help.

⇒ **Connotation.** This theory states that the meaning of a word is simply the set of associations that the word evokes. Think about what connotations the words *spring, bridge,* and *Hawaii* evoke.

⇒ **Denotation.** This theory states that the meaning of a word is not the set of associations it evokes, but rather the entity to which it refers; that is, its denotation or referent. Think about what denotation the words *spring, bridge,* and *Hawaii* have.

⇒ **Extension and Intension.** This theory attempts to combine the first two. Extension refers to the referent of a word, and intension to the associations it evokes. Thus, the meaning of a word includes both its extension and its intension.

⇒ **Componential Analysis.** This theory is based on the idea that meaning can be decomposed into smaller semantic units. These units of meaning are called features. Semantic features can be combined to group entities into classes. For example, the semantic features [+living, +human, -adult] gives us the category of children. Think about how you might decompose the meaning of the words *spring, bridge*, and *Hawaii* into semantic features.

Componential analysis allows us to make generalizations. For example, features of a verb's meaning can be relevant when it comes to choosing the phrases to go along with that verb to form a verb phrase.

Think... What difficulties do connotation, denotation, extension, intension, and componential analysis have in determining the meaning of the words *spring*, *bridge*, and *Hawaii*?

Practice! Practice!

1. For each of the following words, attempt to define their meaning according to the theories of connotation, denotation, and extension and intension.

   a. summer
   b. a linguistics instructor
   c. grass

2. Identify the types of phrases with which the verbs in A and B can occur. What difference in meaning between the verbs in A and the verbs in B determines the type of complement the verbs require?

A	**B**
sweep	crawl
kick	fell

3. Examine the following two groups of words and determine the semantic feature(s) each group has in common. What semantic feature(s) are different between members of each group? What about between the two groups?

Group A:	grandmother	/ mother	/ daughter	/ widow
Group B:	grandfather	/ father	/ son	/ widower

Now... try doing a componential analysis for:
⇒ ewe and lamb
⇒ mare, filly, and colt

What difficulties did you have in decomposing the meanings of the nouns?

CONCEPTS

Linguists use the term 'concepts' to refer to the system we use to identify, classify, and organize all elements of our many and varied experiences. Our conceptual system reveals how meaning is expressed through language.

⇒ **Fuzzy Concepts.** Fuzzy concepts are concepts which can differ from person to person. They have no clear boundaries. Think about how much something has to cost before you would consider it expensive.

⇒ **Graded Membership.** Concepts have internal structure. The members of a concept can be graded according to how typical they are within that concept. The most typical member is selected as the prototype. Other members are arranged around the prototype with members sharing more properties closer to the prototype. Members sharing fewer properties are farther from the prototype. Think... Does the concept of *house* have a graded membership? If so, what might the prototype be? Could this prototype vary from person to person?

⇒ **Metaphor.** The concepts expressed by language do not exist in isolation, but are interconnected and associated. Metaphors, the understanding of one concept in terms of another, can be used to make these connections. Metaphors can be based on our perceptions, our physical experiences, our culture, and on feelings that we share. Think of a metaphor that attributes animal-like properties to people. What might be the basis of such a metaphor?

Exercise! Exercise! For each of the following concepts, determine whether they are fuzzy or graded.

1. cats
2. mountains
3. time
4. vegetables

For any of the above that exhibit a graded membership, determine the member which is prototypical for you. How might this differ from person to person?

Languages can differ in terms of how they choose to express different concepts. This can be done using processes of lexicalization and grammaticalization.

⇒ **Lexicalization.** Lexicalization refers to the process whereby concepts (e.g. snow, light) are encoded into the meanings of words. Languages may differ in terms of how many words they use to convey a concept. How concepts are encoded also varies from language to language. See **Tables 6.9, 6.10,** and **6.11** on **pgs. 203, 204,** and **205** of the text for some examples of systematic differences in how motion is encoded into English, French, and Atsugewi verbs.

⇒ **Grammaticalization.** Grammaticalization refers to concepts which are expressed as affixes or functional categories. See **Table 6.12** on **pg. 206** of the text for some examples of concepts in English that have been grammaticalized. Concepts that are grammaticalized can vary from language to language. See **Table 6.13** on **pg. 206** of the text for an example in Hidatsa in which evidence for the truth of a statement has been grammaticalized. Think about the different ways in which negation has been grammaticalized in English.

Try this!

1. Quite often, languages contain different forms of grammaticalized affixes or functional categories. Consider the data below from Cree involving possession and answer the questions that follow.

	Noun	My Noun	Gloss
1.	mispiton	nispiton	arm
2.	ʧima:n	niʧima:n	canoe
3.	miski:sik	niski:sik	eye
4.	mo:htawiya	no:htawiya	father
5.	mo:ka:wiya	no:ka:wiya	mother
6.	astotin	nitastotin	cap

What are the two different (morphological) ways of indicating possession? What is the semantic basis for this difference? Try to relate it to different kinds of possession: which of the above could you give away and which couldn't you?

2. The language data below illustrates differences in the use of singular and plural prefixes in Swahili. Group the nouns into classes based on their use of the different prefixes. What is the semantic basis for your grouping?

	sg.	**pl.**	**Gloss**
1.	mtoto	watoto	child
2.	mhindi	mihindi	corn
3.	kikombe	vikombe	hair
4.	mkindu	mikindu	date palm
5.	mfigili	mifigili	radish
6.	mwalimu	wawalimu	teacher
7.	kioo	vioo	mirror
8.	mume	waume	husband
9.	kikapu	vikapu	basket
10.	mboga	miboga	pumpkin

3. **German.** German neuter nouns can occur in a prepositional phrase in either the dative case (definite article **dem**) or in the accusative case (definite article **das**). Examine the following sentences and determine the semantic basis for the choice of either the dative or accusative case.

    1. Monika arbeitet in dem Kaffeehaus. (Monika works in the coffeehouse.)
       Stefan kommt in das Kaffeehause. (Stefan comes into the coffeehouse.)

    2. Ritas Stuhl steht neben dem Fenster. (Rita's stool stands next to the window.)
       Jan stellt seinen Stuhl neben das Fenster. (Jan puts his chair next to the window.)

    3. Ein Schuh steht unter dem Bett. (A shoe is under the bed.)
       Kurt stellt den anderen Schuh unter das Bett. (Kurt puts the other shoe under the bed.)

    4. Ilsa ist in dem Wohnzimmer. (Ilsa is in the living-room.)
       Armin geht in das Wohnzimmer. (Armin goes into the living-room.)

    What concept is contained in the German articles that is not found in English articles?

THE ROLE OF SYNTAX

Not only do the words and phrases that make up a sentence contribute to its meaning, but the position of words and phrases in the syntactic structure also has a role.

The contribution of syntax to sentence interpretation includes constructional meaning, structural ambiguity, thematic roles, and pronoun interpretation.

Constructional Meaning

⇒ The meaning of a sentence goes beyond the meaning of the individual words and phrases that comprise it. The syntactic structure, or construction, also contributes to the meaning of the sentence.

⇒ Two common constructions are

- The caused-motion construction: X causes Y to go somewhere
- The ditransitive construction: X causes Y to have Z

Think... What construction is found in the sentence *Joe sold Sabrina a car*? What about in the sentence *Joe flew the airplane to Red Deer*? Is there anything in the verb that implies 'caused motion'? What about 'causes another person to have something'? If not, then where do these meanings come from?

Structural Ambiguity

Structural ambiguity occurs when a group of words in a sentence can be combined in more than one way. Each different combination is associated with a different meaning. Ambiguity can be found in both noun and verb phrases.

⇒ **Noun Phrases.** In the sentence *The surface was painted with red flowers and leaves*, the noun phrase *red flowers and leaves* can be combined in two ways. Each combination corresponds to a particular syntactic structure and meaning.

Meaning One: Both the flowers and the leaves are red.

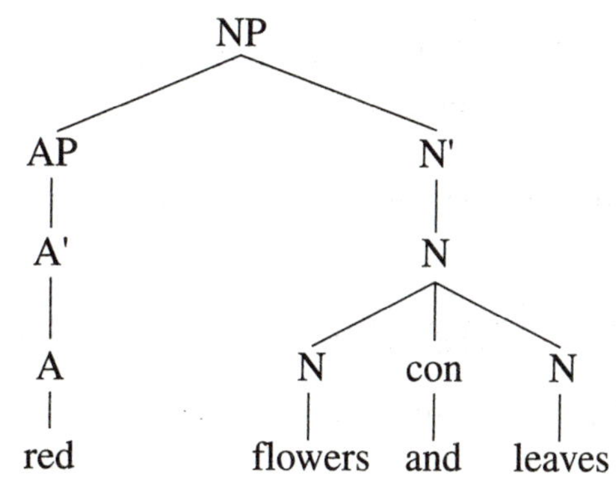

Meaning Two: Only the flowers are red.

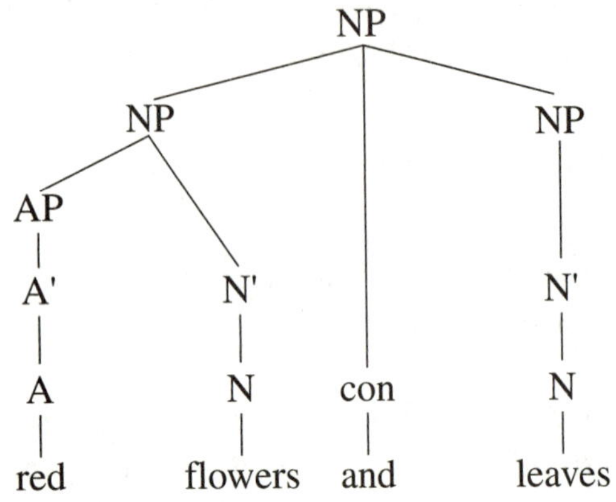

⇒ **Verb Phrases.** In the sentence *Sam ate the cake in the kitchen,* the verb phrase *ate the cake in the kitchen* can be grouped together in two ways. As with noun phrases, each grouping corresponds to a particular syntactic structure and meaning.

Meaning One: Sam ate the cake that was in the kitchen.

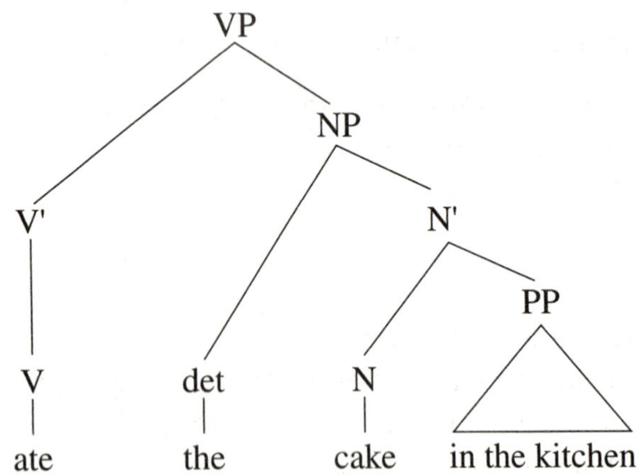

Meaning Two: Sam was in the kitchen eating cake.

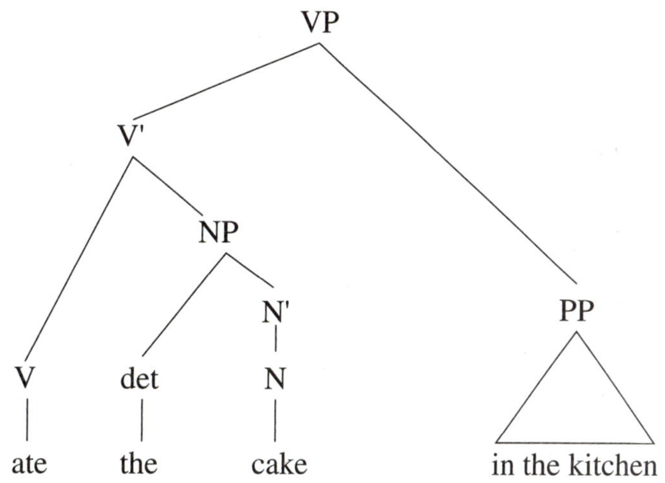

Remember... A sentence can also be lexically ambiguous. This type of ambiguity results from one word in the sentence having more than one meaning. Think about the ambiguity in the sentence *The glasses are on the table.* Which word has more than one meaning? What are the two different meanings? Why would we typically not notice this ambiguity during a conversation?

Each of the sentences below is either lexically or structurally ambiguous. Remember lexical ambiguity comes from a single word, while structural ambiguity comes from more than one possible combination of a group of words.

Try this!

1. Cool beer and wine are what we want.
2. I met the woman standing by the water cooler.
3. Parliament passed a dangerous drug bill.
4. Businessmen like black and white ties.
5. George and Harry or Fred will draw the picture.
6. I want to look at the pictures in the attic.
7. The instructor left his key in the office.

Now... go back over the sentences, and for all those that are structurally ambiguous, draw a tree structure for each possible interpretation, or meaning. You might want to start by first identifying which phrase contains the ambiguity. Remember that each interpretation will have a different structure!

Thematic Roles

To interpret sentences, we need to know who is doing the action, what is undergoing the action, the starting point of the action, etc. Thematic, or theta, roles capture the relations between a sentence and the event it describes.

There are three important properties of thematic roles.

⇒ **Common Thematic Roles.** Some of the common thematic roles include

- Agent (the entity performing the action)
- Theme (the entity undergoing the action)
- Source (the starting point of a movement)
- Goal (the end point of a movement)
- Location (the place where an action occurs)

Think... What thematic role would be assigned to the noun phrases in the sentence *The gardener planted flowers by the front door*? What about the noun phrases in the sentence *John drove the car to Vancouver*? Does a sentence have to contain all the thematic roles outlined above?

⇒ **Thematic Role Assignment.** Thematic roles are assigned to noun phrases based on their position within the sentence. Typically, verbs and prepositions assign thematic roles.

- A verb assigns the agent role (if it has one) to its subject noun phrase.
- A verb assigns the theme role (if it has one) to its complement noun phrase.
- A preposition assigns a thematic role to its complement noun phrases. The specific role that is assigned depends on the specific preposition.

Knowledge of the thematic roles that individual verbs and prepositions assign is stored in our mental lexicon.

See **Figures 6.6, 6.7**, and **6.8** on **pgs. 212** and **213** of the text for examples of thematic role assignment by prepositions and verbs.

Think... How do the noun phrases in the sentences *The gardener planted flowers by the front door* and *John drove the car to Vancouver* receive their thematic roles?

⇒ **Thematic Roles and Deep Structure.** Thematic roles are assigned at deep structure. Remember from the syntax chapter that the operation Move can move a noun phrase from the position it is in as a result of the operation Merge. A noun phrase's position in the syntactic structure that is the result of Merge determines its thematic role. So, if Move has taken place, this operation must first be undone. For example, the wh-question *What should George buy at the store?* has the deep structure *George should buy what at the store.* Accordingly, the verb *buy* assigns the agent role to *George* and the theme role to *what.* Think... Does *what* retain this role after the Move operation changes its position in the structure? How does *the store* receive its thematic role? What is this thematic role?

Exercise! For each of the following sentences, identify all the noun phrases and the thematic role assigned to each noun phrase.

1. Sarah drove that bus from Toronto to St. John's.
2. The children are eating their ice-cream with spoons.
3. Which shoes did you buy at the store?
4. The cat was chased around the garden by a large dog.
5. The boys walked to the park.
6. Sally mailed her nephew a parcel.
7. What did Bill leave at your house?
8. The letter was sent.
9. Ginger scribbled her address on the paper with a pen.
10. The minister is in the pulpit.

Now… go back through each sentence and for each thematic role, determine the verb or preposition that assigned the role. Make sure you put any sentences in which Move has applied into the deep structure first. Remember: the deep structure is the result of Merge.

Pronoun Interpretation

Pronouns replace, or stand for, a noun phrase. This noun phrase is called the antecedent, and it is this antecedent which determines how the pronoun is interpreted. Think… what is the antecedent of the pronoun *she* in the sentence *Janice's sister bought the dress that she liked*? Could *she* refer to *Janice*? How about *Janice's sister*? Could *she* refer to someone else not mentioned in the sentence? What about the pronoun *herself* in the sentence *Janice's sister wondered if Fiona liked herself*? Does *herself* refer to *Fiona*, *Janice,* or *Janice's sister*? Can *herself* refer to someone not mentioned in the sentence?

It is the syntactic structure of the sentence which helps determine which noun phrase can or cannot function as the antecedent of a pronoun. The following concepts are important in understanding how the syntactic structure does this for pronominals and reflexive pronouns.

⇒ **Pronominals and Reflexives.** English pronominals and reflexives vary in terms of number (singular and plural), person (1st, 2nd, and 3rd), and gender (masculine, feminine, and neuter) in the 3rd person. See **Table 6.16** on **pg. 215** of the text for a complete list of the pronominals and reflexives found in English. For example, *she* is a pronominal (3rd person, singular, feminine) and *herself* is a reflexive (3rd person, singular, feminine).

⇒ **C-Command.** The interpretation of pronominals and reflexive pronouns is based on the idea of c-command. A noun phrase c-commands another noun phrase if it is found in the following structure.

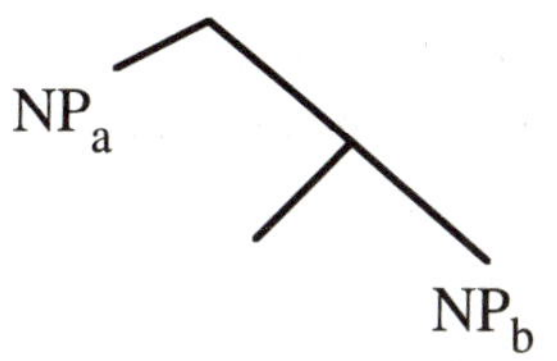

NP_a c-commands NP_b since the first category above NP_a (as indicated by the branching structure) contains NP_b.

⇒ **Principles.** Two principles of interpretation are relevant. The first applies to reflexive pronouns, and the second to pronominals. Notice that these principles are opposite to each other.

- Principle A. This principle applies to reflexive pronouns, and states that a reflexive pronoun must have an antecedent that c-commands it in the same minimal IP. A minimal IP is simply the smallest IP containing the pronoun.

See **Figure 6.12** on **pg. 216** of the text for an illustration of how this principle determines which NPs can and cannot serve as an antecedent for a reflexive pronoun. Essentially, if a NP c-commands a reflexive, the NP can serve as the reflexive's antecedent. Conversely, if a NP does not c-command a reflexive, the NP cannot serve as the reflexive's antecedent.

- Principle B. This principle applies to pronominals, and states that a pronominal cannot have an antecedent that c-commands it in the same minimal IP. Again, a minimal IP is simply the smallest IP containing the pronoun.

See **Figure 6.13** on **pg. 217** of the text for an illustration of how this principle determines which NPs can and cannot serve as antecedents for a pronominal. Essentially, if a NP c-commands a pronominal, the NP cannot serve as the pronominal's antecedent. If a NP does not c-command a pronominal, the NP can serve as the pronominal's antecedent.

Try This! Draw a tree diagram for the sentence *Janice's sister bought the dress that she liked* and for the sentence *Janice's sister wondered if Fiona liked herself.* Use the following structure in both sentences for the NP *Janice's sister.*

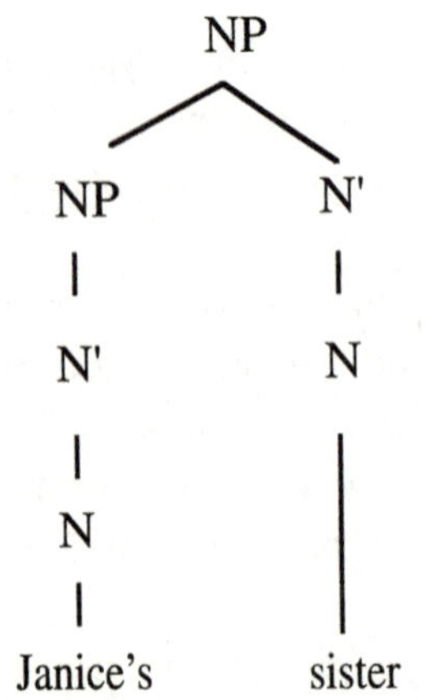

For each NP, determine whether it can or cannot function as the antecedent for the pronoun contained in the sentence. For each, state why it can or cannot function as the antecedent for the specific pronoun. You might want to start by determining whether the pronoun is a pronominal or reflexive. Remember Principle A is for reflexive interpretation and Principle B for pronominal interpretation.

REMINDER! REMINDER!

The interpretation of a sentence involves many factors. Both the syntactic structure and the meaning of the words in that structure contribute to the meaning of a sentence. The construction in which words occur may also contribute to the meaning of the sentence. As well, the role each NP in a sentence plays must be interpreted. And, when words in a sentence can be combined in more than one way, ambiguity results!

PRAGMATICS

Besides the structure of a sentence and the thematic roles assigned to the noun phrases within a sentence, there are many other factors involved in sentence interpretation. Pragmatics is the study of the role other necessary information has in sentence interpretation.

⇒ **Beliefs and Attitudes.** Non-linguistic knowledge can be used to interpret elements within a sentence. Think about the sentence *City Council denied the demonstrators a permit because they advocated violence*. Does the pronoun *they* refer to the demonstrators or the council members? Think about how the pronoun reference changes if we change the verb from *advocate* to *abhor*. Who does the pronoun refer to now? How is this difference in pronoun reference related to our beliefs about demonstrators and council members?

⇒ **Presupposition.** Presupposition refers to the assumption or belief implied by the use of a particular word. Think about the meaning of the sentence *John admitted that the soccer team had won the game* in relation to the meaning of the sentence *John said that the soccer team had won the game*. In which sentence does the verb presuppose, or imply, that the team had actually won?

⇒ **Setting / Deictics.** The form and interpretation of some words depends on the location of the speaker and listener within a particular setting. These words are called deictics. Some examples of English deictics include *here / there* and *this / that. Here* and *this* are used to refer to items close to the speaker, while *there* and *that* are used to refer to words close to the listener. See **Table 6.17** on **pg. 219** of the text for some examples of how deictic distinctions can vary across languages.

⇒ **Discourse / Topic.** Many sentences can only be interpreted in reference to information contained in preceding sentences. **Discourse** is the term used to describe the connected series of utterances. Old (given) information refers to knowledge that speakers assume addressees know, while new information refers to knowledge that is being introduced into the discourse for the first time. **Topic** refers to what a sentence or portion of the discourse is about. Some languages (e.g., Japanese) use a marker to indicate the topic of the discourse.

Practice! Practice! Sentences can be difficult to interpret because they are ungrammatical, because they violate our knowledge of the world, or because they contain words which have no known referent. For each of the following sentences, identify why it is hard to interpret.

1. Our ten-month-old son is six feet tall.
2. Mike red bought car a.
3. Palm trees grow vigorously at the North Pole.
4. Radiculus glautons are found in the soil.
5. The bumble-bee picked up the cat and flew back to the hive with it.

Now... reconsider sentence 4. What meaning might you assign to the unknown words in this sentence? What might be the meaning of the overall sentence?

Why might the sentence *His mother wants you to be a doctor* be difficult to interpret if it is not part of a discourse (i.e., as a stand-alone sentence)?

CONVERSATION

We use words and sentences to convey messages. And we often do this by having a conversation with someone. Conversations have rules. These rules refer to our understanding of how language is used to convey messages. Our knowledge of these rules also contributes to our interpretation of utterances.

⇒ **Cooperative Principle.** This is the general principle guiding all conversations. It requires participants (speakers and addressees) to make their contributions to the conversation appropriate to the conversation.

⇒ **Specific Maxims.** Conversations also have more specific guidelines. These guidelines are called specific maxims, and if we follow these maxims, then we have adhered to the Cooperative Principle.

- Maxim of Relation (Make your contribution relevant)
- Maxim of Quality (Make your contribution truthful)
- Maxim of Quantity (Make your contribution only as informative as required)
- Maxim of Manner (Make your contribution unambiguous, clear and logical)

⇒ **Conversational Implicature.** During the course of a conversation, we are often able to make inferences about what is meant, but was not actually said. Consider, for example, the following interaction:

Mike: How did you do on the last exam?
Jim: Want to come with me to the Registrar's Office?

Think about which Conversational Maxim Jim has violated. What can you infer about how Jim did on the exam even though he doesn't actually tell Mike how he did?

Try This!!

You've just missed your bus and are standing at the bus-stop waiting for the next bus. The time is 2 PM and the next bus is due at 2:15 PM, but you don't know that. You ask someone at the bus-stop when the next bus is due and receive several replies. Each reply you receive may or may not violate one or more conversational maxims. For each reply, identify which maxim(s), if any, have been violated.

1. When's the next bus?
   At 2:30. (He's lying.)

   ____

2. When's the next bus?
   When I was little I was obsessed with buses. I wanted to be a bus-driver. I had hundreds of different kinds of buses. Little buses, big buses, red buses, blue buses and even double-deckered buses. Did you know that in England, many buses are double-deckered? I have made a study of buses. I think the next bus will be here in 15 minutes. Did you know that in India there are no buses? Did you know I wanted to be a bus driver? Did you know …

   ____

3. When's the next bus?
   Let me think! If the last bus was here at 1:50 and if they run every 20 minutes or so, then the next bus should be here at 2:10. (He has no idea.)

   ____

4. When's the next bus?
   At 2:15, but if we were in Newfoundland that would be 2:45.

   ____

5. When's the next bus?
   I don't know. (He's telling the truth.)

   ____

REVIEW! REVIEW! Make sure you can:

- identify the semantic relations between words (4)
- identify the semantic relations between sentences (3)
- define connotation, denotation, extension and intension
- do componential analysis
- spot fuzzy concepts, grammaticalized concepts, and lexicalized concepts
- spot the semantic basis for different word classes
- spot lexical ambiguity
- spot and represent structural ambiguity
- identify noun phrases and their thematic roles
- identify the effect of world knowledge in sentence interpretation
- identify when presupposition occurs in sentence interpretation
- spot the different forms of deictic terms
- identify conversational principles and maxims

QUESTIONS? PROBLEMS? DIFFICULTIES?

CHAPTER 7. HISTORICAL LINGUISTICS: THE STUDY OF LANGUAGE CHANGE

Historical Linguistics studies the principles governing language change, including both its description and explanation. Some of the important topics and concepts in this chapter include:

1. Phonetic Sound Change
2. Phonological Change
3. Morphological Change
4. Syntactic Change
5. Lexical Change
6. Semantic Change
7. Language Reconstruction
8. The discovery of Indo-European
9. Naturalness and Typology

LANGUAGE CHANGE

Some important points concerning language change include:

⇒ Language is always changing. However, for a particular change to take hold, it must be accepted by the language community as a whole.

⇒ Language change is regular and systematic. Some changes affect all words without exception. Other changes begin in a small number of words in the speech of a small number of speakers. These changes may gradually spread through both the vocabulary and the population.

⇒ Languages change because of the way language is acquired. Children are not born with a complete grammar, but must construct a grammar based on the language they are exposed to. Therefore, changes will occur from one generation to the next, and because all children have the same genetic capabilities for language, and construct their grammars in similar fashions, the same patterns of change repeat both within and across languages.

⇒ Causes of language change include articulatory simplification (see **Table 7.2** on **pg. 231** of the text for some examples), spelling pronunciation, reanalysis, analogy, and borrowing as a result of language contact. Hypercorrections (overgeneralizations about a particular rule) can also cause languages to change.

SEQUENTIAL SOUND CHANGE

While all aspects of a language's structure can change, sound change is often the most noticeable. There are many types of sound change that can occur; however, most sound changes involve sequences of segments. The major types of sequential sound changes are outlined in the boxes below.

⇒ **Assimilation.** Assimilation involves sounds changing to become more like the nearby sounds. Assimilation increases the efficiency of the articulations involved in producing the sequence of sounds. Such an increase in efficiency can result in articulatory simplification.

Some common examples include:

Assimilation Processes

a. Place of Articulation Assimilation
A sound becomes similar to a nearby sound in terms of place of articulation. See **Table 7.4** on **pg. 234** of the text for some examples.

b. Manner of Articulation Assimilation
A consonant changes its manner of articulation to be like a nearby sound. See **Table 7.5** on **pg. 234** of the text for some examples.

c. Total Assimilation
A sound assimilates totally to a following sound. See **Table 7.6** on **pg. 235** of the text for some examples.

d. Palatalization
A non-palatal sound becomes or moves toward a palatal sound. This usually occurs near a sound that is made with the tongue at or near the hard palate—usually [y] or [i]. Palatalization is often the first step in the process of creating an affricate (called affrication) from a stop. See **Table 7.7** on **pg. 235** of the text for some examples.

e. Nasalization
A vowel becomes nasal near a nasal sound. See **Table 7.8** on **pg. 235** of the text for some examples.

Remember..... Assimilation most often affects adjacent segments. It can, however, apply at a distance. Umlaut, which is responsible for irregular plurals such as goose/geese, is an example of such an assimilatory process. See **Table 7.9** on **pg. 236** of the text for some more examples of this process.

⇒ **Weakening and Deletion.** Sounds, both vowels and consonants, tend to weaken over time. They can also delete. Deletion is often the end result of the weakening process.

- Full vowels have a tendency to weaken, or reduce, to a schwa-like vowel. Vowels are often subject to deletion when they occur in unstressed syllables.

  Vowels weakening and deletion processes include:

Vowel Weakening	**Vowel Deletion**
a. Vowel Reduction An unstressed vowel reduces to schwa.	a. Apocope The deletion of a word final vowel. b. Syncope The deletion of a word internal vowel

  See **Table 7.14** on **pg. 238** and **Table 7.15** on **pg. 239** of the text for some examples of the above processes.

- Consonants tend to weaken along a path determined by the hierarchy shown below.

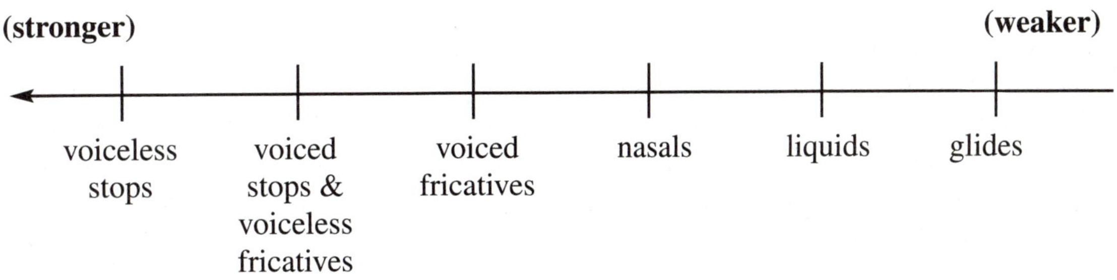

Think… which is stronger? [t] or [s]? [t] or [d]? [tt] or [t]? [s] or [z]? [s] or [ss]? [v] or [f]? Remember, geminate (long) consonants are stronger than their non-geminate counterparts.

Consonantal weakening and deletion processes include:

Consonantal Weakening	**Consonantal Deletion**
a. Degemination A long sound becomes short. This is usually the first step in the weakening of consonants. b. Frication A stop weakens to a fricative. This often occurs between vowels. c. Voicing Voiceless stops or fricatives weaken to voiced stops or fricatives d. Rhotacism A fairly common type of weakening in which [z] weakens to [r].	a. Consonantal Deletion Consonants often delete when they occur as part of a consonant cluster, or as the final consonant in a word, or as the last step after several weakening processes. See **Table 7.16** on **pg. 239** of the text for some examples.

See **Table 7.17** on **pg. 240** of the text for an example of Degemination, Frication, and Voicing in Romance and **Table 7.18** on **pg. 241** of the text for some examples of Rhotacism.

Remember…. It is most common for consonants to weaken over time. However, consonants can also strengthen. For example, glides often strengthen to an affricate. This process is called Glide Strengthening and is common in word initial position. See **Table 7.19** on **pg. 241** of the text for some examples.

⇒ **Others.** There are other types of sound changes as well, many of which will be familiar to you from the Phonology chapter! These types of sound changes are not as frequent as those already presented, but like assimilation also tend to have the overall effect of making sequences of sounds easier to articulate. Also like assimilation, these changes can affect adjacent segments or segments at a distance.

Some common examples include:

Other Processes

a. Dissimilation
A sound becomes less like a nearby sound. This often occurs so that a sequence of sounds is easer to articulate or perceive.

b. Epenthesis
A sound is inserted. This usually occurs to break up a consonant cluster that is hard to pronounce. See **Table 7.10** on **pg. 236** of the text for some examples from Old English and **Table 7.12** on **pg. 237** for some examples from Romance.

c. Metathesis
The position of two sounds has changed relative to each other. See **Table 7.13** on **pg. 237** of the text for some examples from Old English.

OTHER TYPES OF SOUND CHANGE

The changes considered so far have all involved segments changing under the influence of nearby, although not necessarily adjacent, segments. There are two other common types of sound change: segmental and auditory.

⇒ **Segmental Change.** Segmental change involves a change within the segment itself. Segmental change often involves affricates. Affricates are considered a complex segment, since they consist of a stop and a fricative, and complex segments often simplify over time.

One common example is given below:

Segmental Change Processes

a. Deaffrication
An affricate becomes a fricative by eliminating the stop portion of the affricate. See **Table 7.20** and **Table 7.21** on **pg. 241** for an example of this process in the change from Old French to French and how this process influenced the pronunciation of French words borrowed into English.

⇒ **Auditory Change.** In addition to the articulatory considerations typically involved in sound change, auditory factors can also have an influence.

One common example is given below:

Auditory Change Processes

a. Substitution

One segment is replaced with a similar sounding segment. See **Table 7.22** on **pg. 242** of the text for an example in the change from Middle English to English.

Get ready to identify sound changes …

NAME THAT SOUND CHANGE

Each of the following exemplifies one or more sound changes. The older form is on the left, and the more recent form on the right. Identify the sound change that has taken place for each of the underlined sound(s).

1. Proto-Quechua [cumpi] > Tena [cumbi]

 ____

2. Old English [hlaf] > Modern English [lof]

 ____

3. Latin [mare] > Portuguese [mar]

 ____

4. Proto-Slavic [kemerai] > Russian [tʃemer]

 ____

5. Proto-Tupi-Guarani [puʔam] > Guarani [puʔã]

 ____

6. Latin [ornamentum] > Old French [ornəment]

7. Old English [knotta] > Mod. English [nɑt]

8. Proto-Germanic [doːmaz] > Old Icelandic [doːmr]

9. Latin [venre] > Spanish [vendre]

10. Early Latin [inpossibiliss] > Latin [impossibilis]

11. Proto-Bantu [mukiːpa] > Swahili [mʃipa]

12. Proto-Romance [sekuru] > Spanish [seguru]

13. Latin [pekkatum] > [pekaθo] > [pekaðo]

14. Proto-Romance [biskɔktu] > Latin [biskotto]

Now... Sound change tends to occur in a step-by-step fashion, so a single sound can often be subject to a number of different sound changes. But, these multiple sound changes are often not visible in the resulting form.

Examine the change below that affected the word 'good' in the development from Proto-Germanic to Old Icelandic and see if you can identify all the changes, including any intermediate but not visible changes that have affected the underlined sounds.

Proto-Germanic [goːdas] Old Icelandic [goːðr]

PHONOLOGICAL SOUND CHANGE

The sound changes described in the previous sections can influence a language's phonological inventory. That is, they can add, eliminate, or rearrange the phonemes within a language.

⇒ **Phonological Splits.** A phonological split adds phonemes to a language's phonological inventory. In a phonological split, allophones of the same phoneme come to contrast with each other. This is often caused by a loss of the conditioning environment. That is, sounds that were once predictable are no longer predictable, and are, therefore, phonemic.

Consider the following example in the development of English.

Old English: In Old English, /n/ had two allophones:
– [ŋ] occurred before velar stops
– [n] occurred elsewhere

So … a word like 'sing' was pronounced as [sɪŋg].

Middle English: Consonant Deletion applied to remove [g] at the end of a word (after a nasal consonant). This created a minimal pair between 'sing', now pronounced as [siŋ], and 'sin', pronounced as [sɪn]. And minimal pairs tell us that sounds contrast.

This split can be diagrammed as follows:

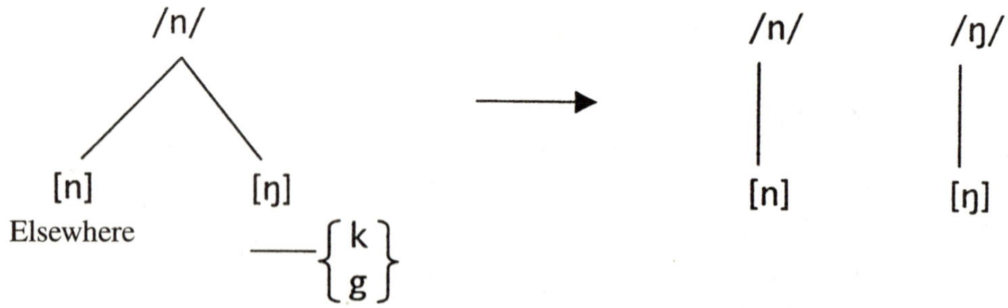

What phoneme was added to the language?

Think… Spelling often lags behind sound change. We still spell 'sing' with the final 'g' even though it is now silent. Many silent letters in our English spelling system are a reflection of older pronunciations!

⇒ **Phonological Mergers.** While a phonological split adds phonemes to a language, a phonological merger reduces the number of contrasts.

A good example of a phonological merger comes from Cockney English. In Cockney English, the interdental and labiodental fricatives have merged. That is, all instances of [θ] and [ð] have become [f] and [v] respectively. Think . . . what phonemes have been lost from the phonemic inventory?

⇒ **Phonological Shifts.** A phonological shift does not add to or diminish a language's phonemic inventory. Rather, some of the phonemes are reorganized with respect to each other.

The Great English Vowel Shift, beginning in Middle English, is a well-known example of a phonological shift affecting vowels. The chart below gives the Middle English long vowels before the vowel shift occurred.

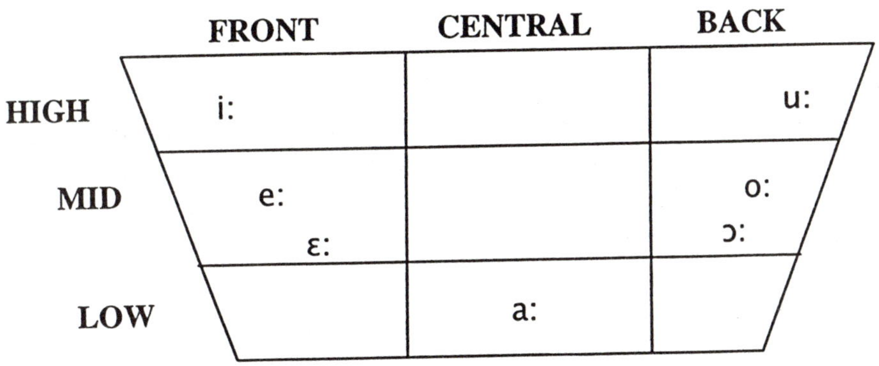

The Great English Vowel Shift affected the long vowels. It probably began with the diphthongization of [i] and [u]. The creation of the diphthongs [aj] and [aw] reduced the number of simple vowels from seven to five. The remaining vowels then shifted upwards in their articulation.

The vowel shifts are summarized below.

1. Long [i] became the diphthong [aj]
2. Long [u] became the diphthong [aw]
3. Long [e] became [i]
4. Long [ɛ] became [i]
5. Long [a] became [e]
6. Long [o] became [u]
7. Long [ɔ] became [o]

And as the vowels shifted, length was lost. After the Great English Vowel Shift, the long vowels now looked like:

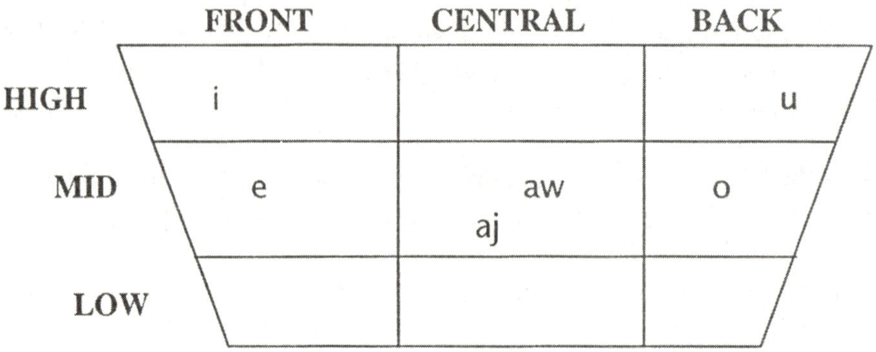

Compare the two vowel charts. What was the overall effect of the vowel shift in terms of the number of vowels?

Think ... Many of our vowel spellings reflect Middle English pronunciation. For example, the word 'goose' is spelled with 'oo' because this orthographic symbol represented [o:]. 'goose' continues to be spelled this way, even though as a result of the Great English Vowel Shift [o:] became [u], changing the pronunciation of 'goose' to [gus]. One reason for this mismatch between spelling and pronunciation is that spelling was standardized before the vowels had finished shifting!

Try this! For each of the Middle English words below, state the vowel change that would have occurred as a result of the Great Vowel Shift, and then give the spelling of corresponding Modern English word.

Middle English	Vowel Change	Modern English Word
[no:n]	________________	________________
[li:fə]	________________	________________
[swe:t]	________________	________________
[bɔ:st]	________________	________________
[gu:n]	________________	________________

Phonological Shifts can also affect consonants. One famous example is Grimm's Law, which is actually comprised of three sound changes.

In 1822, Jacob Grimm (of Grimm's Fairy Tales) noticed some regular sound correspondences between the Germanic languages and the non-Germanic Indo-European languages. The correspondences he noticed are listed below.

Non-Germanic Consonant	As in these Non-Germanic Words	Corresponding Germanic Consonant	As in these Germanic Cognates
[p]	**p**ater (Latin)	[f]	**f**ather (German – **V**ater)
[t]	**t**onare (Latin)	[θ]	**th**under
[k]	**c**anis (Latin)	[x] → [h]	**h**ound (German – **H**und)
[b]	kanna**b**is (Greek)	[p]	hem**p**
[d]	**d**uo (Latin)	[t]	**t**wo
[g]	a**g**er (Latin)	[k]	a**c**re
[bh]	**bh**rata (Sanskrit)	[b]	**b**rother (German – Bruder)
[dh]	vi**dh**ava (Sanskrit)	[d]	wi**d**ow
[gh]	**gh**ansas (Sanskrit)	[g]	**g**oose (German – Gans)

Grimm explained these correspondences using three sound changes.

(1) Voiceless stops became voiceless fricatives (i.e., weakening – frication)

PIE		Proto-Germanic (PG)
[p]	>	[f]
[t]	>	[θ]
[k]	>	[x] → [h]

(2) Voiced stops became voiceless stops

PIE		PG
[b]	>	[p]
[d]	>	[t]
[g]	>	[k]

(3) Voiced aspirated stops became voiced unaspirated stops

PIE		PG
[bh]	>	[b]
[dh]	>	[d]
[gh]	>	[g]

The first of Grimm's rules involves the weakening of stops to fricatives. This, of course, is a phonetically plausible sound change. The result of this weakening process left Proto-Germanic without voiceless stops. Since it is rare for a language to completely lack voiceless stops, this gap was filled by devoicing the voiced stops. The re-introduction of voiceless stops in turn created a lack of voiced stops. This new gap was filled by de-aspirating the voiced aspirated stops. This, of course, created yet another gap: a lack of voiced aspirated stops. This gap was not filled!

There are exceptions to Grimm's Law. Some exceptions can be traced back to borrowings from Latin and French. Such borrowings did not undergo Grimm's Law, since these words entered the language long after the sound shift had occurred.

MORPHOLOGICAL CHANGE

Morphological change affects the structure of words within a language. Morphological change involves either the addition or the loss of affixes. Recall from morphology that affixes are bound morphemes that attach to a base. Affixes provide grammatical information (inflection), or are used to create new words (derivation).

⇒ **The addition of affixes.** Affixes can be added to a language through

- Borrowing
- Grammaticalization (creating new grammatical forms from lexical forms)
- Fusion (developing an affix from two words that are frequently adjacent to each other). See **Table 7.28** on **pg. 247** of the text for some examples from English, and **Table 7.29** on **pg. 247** for some examples from Italian.

⇒ **The loss of affixes.** Affixes can also be lost through

- Lack of use. See **Table 7.30** on **pg. 248** of the text for some English examples.
- Sound Change. See **Table 7.32** on **pg. 249** of the text for an example of how sound changes caused the loss of Old English case affixes.

The effect of adding or losing affixes. The loss of affixes can result in a synthetic morphological system becoming analytic, while the addition of affixes can result in an analytic morphological system gradually becoming synthetic. An analytic language has very few inflectional affixes (e.g., Modern English). In contrast, a synthetic language has many inflectional affixes (e.g., Old English).

Try This! Folk Etymology is used to refer to the analysis of a word based on an incorrect historical division of that word into its apparent morphemes. This is usually done without reference to the word's origins. Hence the use of the word 'folk'! See **Table 7.34** on **pg. 250** of the text for some English examples.

Identify the base and affix for each of the following words.

- yearling
- duckling
- gosling

- underling
- hireling
- nursling

Are the words in the second column as common as those in the first? Do they have the same meaning?

Historically, each of the above words consists of a base plus the affix –ing. This German affix has the meaning 'having the quality of'. What has happened to this affix in terms of its form? Why would such a reanalysis occur? What happened to the affix in terms of its meaning? What might have caused this shift?

What about the word *earthling*? How does this relate to the original German affix as well as the above words? What about the word *darling*?

QUICK REMINDER

Reanalysis and analogy can also affect the morphological structure of a language. Reanalysis adds new morphemes to a language, while analogy can change an existing morphological pattern. See **Table 7.35** on **pg. 251** of the text for an example of Reanalysis in the development of English.

SYNTACTIC CHANGE

Change can also affect the syntactic component of a language's grammar. Change often affects the word order patterns found in a language. It can also affect the transformations found within a language.

⇒ **Word Order.** Languages can change their basic word order pattern. One common change involves the change from an SOV (subject-object-verb) order to an SVO (subject-verb-object) order. This is a change that happened in the development of English. English descended from a Germanic language having an SOV order.

⇒ **Transformations.** Yes/no questions in English are formed using the Inversion transformation. In Old English, both main verbs and auxiliary verbs could be inverted. In Modern English, though, only auxiliary verbs can be inverted. Now, any sentence that does not contain an auxiliary must be made into a yes/no question using 'do'.

Try This! Below are some sentences from 16th century English along with their modern counterparts. Examine the sentences, and determine how negatives were formed. How does this differ from today's English?

1. A kinder gentleman treads not the Earth.
   A kinder gentleman doesn't tread the Earth.

2. Hate counsels not in such a quantity.
   Hate doesn't counsel in such a quantity.

3. Clamber not you up to the casement then.
   Don't climb up to the casement then.

CONNECTIONS

Changes can have far-reaching effects. A change that affects the phonology of a language can eventually affect the morphology, which in turn can affect the syntax of a language.

Consider an example (somewhat simplified) from the development of English.

⇒ Old English was a highly inflected language. Old English inflectional affixes included:

1. Case: Nominative, Accusative, Dative, Genitive
2. Number: Singular, Dual, Plural
3. Person: First, Second, Third
4. Gender: Masculine, Feminine, Neuter
5. Tense: Past, Present

Inflectional affixes were found on pronouns, nouns, articles, adjectives, verbs, etc. As in many inflected languages, Old English had a fairly free word order. Sentences with SVO, VSO, and SOV orders could all be found.

⇒ During Middle English, sound changes started happening in unstressed syllables. These sound changes included:

- m → n / ______#
- n → Ø / ______#
- a, o, u, i, e → ə / ______#

These three sound changes affected the inflectional system. Inflectional affixes in Old English were suffixes, and suffixes are typically not stressed.

The following two examples illustrate the application of the above rules and their effect on the Old English inflectional system.

Old English						**Middle English**
foxum	>	foxun	>	foxu	>	foxə
helpan	>	helpan	>	helpa	>	helpə

As a result of these sound changes, all the affixes became the same: 'ə'. Since it was now impossible to tell what information was contained in an affix, the Old English affixes were dropped.

⇒ But, speakers still needed to know what the subject of a sentence was, what the object of a sentence was, and what noun an adjective referred to. To get this information, speakers of English began to …

1. Rely on prepositions.
2. Rely on fixed word order (SVO).

So … sound changes can have a drastic effect on a language's development over time.

> **QUICK REMINDER!**
>
> Just like with phonological rules, sound changes also often require an order to their application. For example, the three rules presented in the last section require some ordering. [m] has to first change to [n] before it can be deleted. If this change does not occur first, then [n] would not delete and the affixes would not all become [ə]. Note that it doesn't matter when the vowel reduction rule applies!

LEXICAL CHANGE

Lexical change involves modifications to the lexicon. There are two main types of lexical change: addition and loss.

<u>Addition of Lexical Items</u>

New lexical items are typically added to a language's vocabulary in one of two ways.

⇒ **Word Formation.** Some of the morphological phenomena found in the Morphology chapter are frequently used to add new words to a language. These new words often fill a lexical gap resulting from technological innovations. Compounding, Derivation, Acronyms, Backformation, Blending, Clipping, and Conversion can all be used to add new words to a language. See **Table 7.38** on **pg. 255** and **Table 7.39** on **pg. 256** of the text for some Old English examples of Compounding and Derivation.

⇒ **Borrowing.** As languages come into contact, they often borrow words from each other. Borrowed words are often called loan words. There are three types of influences that languages can have on each other.

- *Substratum Influence.* This type of influence results in the borrowing of place-names as well as names for unfamiliar objects or items. For example, English borrowed place-names such as Thames, London, and Dover from the Celtic language.

- *Superstratum Influence.* This type of influence often results in borrowings related to all things official. For example, English borrowed many words from the French language during the Middle English period. French loan words are typically found in relation to government, religion, the judiciary, science, culture and warfare. See **Table 7.40** on **pg. 257** for some examples.

- *Adstratum Influence.* Adstratum influence often results in the borrowing of common, everyday words. For example, English borrowed many Scandinavian words, including cake, egg, husband, score, window, and ugly. See **Table 7.42** on **pg. 258** for some examples of the French influnce on Montreal English.

Loss of Lexical Items

Words can also be lost from the vocabulary of a language. Loan words, non-loan words, compounds, and derived words can all be lost. The most common reason for the loss of a lexical item is some societal change that has rendered an object, and therefore its name, obsolete. See **Table 7.46** on **pg. 259** of the text for some words no longer used in English.

SEMANTIC CHANGE

In addition to the addition and loss of lexical items, the meanings of existing words can also change over time. There are seven main types of semantic change.

TYPE	DEFINITION
Broadening	The meaning of a word becomes more general or inclusive over time. See **Table 7.47** on **pg. 260** of the text for some examples.
Narrowing	The meaning of a word becomes less general or inclusive over time. See **Table 7.48** on **pg. 260** of the text for some examples.
Amelioration	The meaning of a word changes to become more positive or favourable. See **Table 7.49** on **pg. 261** of the text for some examples.
Pejoration	The meaning of a word changes to become less positive or favourable. See **Table 7.50** on **pg. 261** of the text for some examples.
Weakening	The meaning of a word weakens over time. See **Table 7.51** on **pg. 261** of the text for some examples.
Semantic Shift	A word loses its former meaning and takes on a new, but related, meaning. See **Table 7.52** on **pg. 261** of the text for some examples.
Metaphor	A word with a concrete meaning takes on a more abstract meaning, without losing the original meaning. See **Table 7.53** on **pg. 263** of the text for some examples.

Practice! Practice! For each of the following words, identify which of the processes in the above table best captures the semantic change that has occurred.

Word	Earlier Meaning	Later Meaning	Semantic Change
1. aisle	passage between pews of a church	passage between rows of seats	________
2. mischievous	disastrous	playfully annoying	________
3. blue	a colour	being melancholy	________
4. spill	shed blood	waste of liquid	________
5. fond	foolish	affectionate	________
6. butler	male servant in charge of the wine cellar	male servant in charge of a household	________
7. passenger	traveller	one who travels by vehicle or vessel	________
8. wretch	exile	unhappy person	________
9. notorious	widely known	widely and unfavourably known	________
10. chair	a seat	head of a university or college department	________

COMPARATIVE RECONSTRUCTION

By comparing languages with each other, it can be determined if they are or are not genetically related. Genetically related languages are languages that have descended from a common ancestor. Using the comparative method, this ancestor can be reconstructed. This is typically done by comparing later forms to determine what the earlier form must have looked like. Although it is possible to reconstruct all aspects of a language's grammar, the focus here is on phonological reconstruction.

Some important terms ...

⇒ **Cognates** are phonetically and semantically similar words that have descended from a common source. Cognates are compared to reconstruct what this common source must have looked like.

⇒ A **proto-language** is a language that has been reconstructed using a comparative method. Written evidence of what this language actually looked like typically doesn't exist.

⇒ A proto-language consists of **proto-forms**. These are the individual reconstructed words of the proto-language. Proto-forms are usually indicated with a (*).

Some important strategies ...

⇒ **The Phonetic Plausibility Strategy** requires that any change posited to account for the differences between the proto-form (the ancestor) and the cognates must be phonetically plausible. That is, a sound change that has been found to occur in the course of language development must be able to account for these differences. For our purposes, the sound changes listed under the heading **sequential change**, as well as under **segmental** and **auditory change**, are all plausible.

⇒ **The Majority Rules Strategy** operates in the absence of a phonetically plausible sound change. This strategy states that when no phonetically plausible sound change can be determined, we may reconstruct the segment that occurs in the majority of the cognates. This strategy should only be used as a last resort.

An example ...

Reconstruct the proto-forms for the data below.

	Lang A	Lang B	Lang C
1.	hauda	hauta	hauta
2.	sav	ʃive	sav

⇒ **First.** Determine the number of sounds that need to be reconstructed. This is straightforward for (1) in that all the cognates have the same number of sounds: five. The situation is different in (2). In (2), two of the cognates contain three sounds, and one contains four. If four sounds are reconstructed, then deletion must have occurred in Lang A and C. If three sounds are reconstructed, then epenthesis must have occurred in Lang B. It is more plausible for deletion rather than epenthesis to occur at the end of words. (2), therefore, requires the reconstruction of four sounds.

⇒ **Second.** Look for any total correspondences. These are sounds which have not changed; they are the same for all the cognates. Reconstruct these sounds. The proto-forms after this step are: *hau?a and *??v?.

⇒ **Third.** Examine alternations between the different languages and determine phonetic plausibility.

- (1) exhibits an alternation between [t] and [d]. Either [t] or [d] can be reconstructed in the proto-form.

  - If [d] is reconstructed, then the change from the proto-form to the form in Lang B ([d] > [t]) does not correspond to a sound change. Therefore, this has a low phonetic plausibility.
  - If [t] is reconstructed, then the change from the proto-form to Lang A and C ([t] > [d]) can be explained as an instance of weakening (a voiceless stop weakens to a voiced stop). This has a high phonetic plausibility.

  Reconstruct the change that has the highest phonetic plausibility. The proto-form therefore becomes *hauta.

- (2) exhibits three alternations. First, consider the alternation between [s] and [ʃ].

  - If [ʃ] is reconstructed, then the change [ʃ] > [s] in Lang A and C has low phonetic plausibility, since it does not correspond to a sound change.
  - If [s] is reconstructed, then the change [s] > [ʃ] in Lang B can be explained as palatalization. Therefore, [s] is reconstructed.

  Second, consider the presence or absence of a word final vowel in the cognates. Recall from above that it is more plausible for a sound to delete then be epenthesized in this position. Therefore, [e] is reconstructed.

  Third, consider the vowel alternation between [a] and [i].

  - If [a] is reconstructed then the change [a] > [i] occurs in Lang B.
  - If [i] is reconstructed, then the opposite change ([i] > [a]) occurs in Lang A and C.

  Neither one corresponds to a sound change, and so both have a low phonetic plausibility. This strategy, therefore, cannot be used to reconstruct this segment. The proto-form, after this step, is *s?ve.

⇒ **Fourth.** Any sounds for which no phonetically plausible sound change could be identified require using the Majority Rules Strategy. In (2), the alternation between [a] and [i] can not be accounted for using a sound change; therefore, [a] is reconstructed since it occurs in the majority of the cognates. The proto-form becomes *save. Notice that this proto-form does not correspond to any of the cognates. This is okay!

⇒ **Fifth.** Put together a summary of the sound changes that have occurred since the different languages split from the proto-language. Remember that the proto-form you have just reconstructed is older than the cognates from the descendent languages. Voicing and Apocope have occurred in the development of Lang A, while only Apocope occurred in the development of Lang C. Palatalization occurred in the development of Lang B.

Something to think about ....

⇒ Sound changes that tend to occur across languages are often referred to as natural. Sound changes that are phonetically plausible are more natural than those which are not. **Naturalness** is important to think about when doing reconstruction, since language change is regular and systematic.

⇒ It is also important to think about universal properties of language when doing reconstruction. This is often referred to as **typological plausibility**. Think about the change from voiced stops to voiceless stops in Grimm's Law (see pgs. 162–164). This change has a low phonetic plausibility and is therefore not a natural sound change. However, this change occurred as weakening (frication) left the language without voiceless stops, which are found in virtually every language. The change from voiced to voiceless stops, therefore, happened for typological reasons.

REMINDER! REMINDER!

In order to do language reconstruction, you need to be able to identify phonetically plausible sound changes. And in order to do this, you need to know the different types of sequential, segmental, and auditory sound changes. Make sure you are very familiar with them!

Practice! Practice! Each data group below contains some cognate sets. Assume that all the cognates are in phonetic transcription and that all members of the cognate set have the same meaning. Reconstruct the proto-forms and list all the sound changes that have taken place in each language. Remember: for some languages there may be no sound changes, while for others there may be multiple sound changes.

While the data is from hypothetical or highly regularized data, it exemplifies processes found in actual languages.

GROUP ONE

	Lang A	Lang B	Proto-Form
1.	mũtə	muθo	* ______________
2.	fumə	vumo	* ______________
3.	pippon	bipona	* ______________
4.	nõk	noga	* ______________
5.	wus	juza	* ______________
6.	fitə	vido	* ______________

Summary of Sound Changes:

Lang A	
Lang B	

Remember … the reconstructed form does not have to be the same as any of the forms found in the descendent languages!

GROUP TWO

	Lang A	Lang B	Lang C	Lang D	**Proto-Form**
1.	puxa	buga	puka	puk	*________
2.	nizudz	nizuz	mizu	nir	*________

Summary of Sound Changes:

Lang A	
Lang B	
Lang C	
Lang D	

GROUP THREE

	Lang A	Lang B	Lang C	Lang D	**Proto-Form**
1.	pika	big	pik	biha	*________
2.	wira	wil	wir	wira	*________
3.	vida	bita	vit	viθa	*________

Summary of Sound Changes:

Lang A	
Lang B	
Lang C	
Lang D	

GROUP FOUR

	Lang A	Lang B	Lang C	**Proto-Form**
1.	tuhu	tuu	tuhu	*__________
2.	nika	nika	nika	*__________
3.	kaza	kasa	kaʃa	*__________
4.	tuku	tuku	tuku	*__________
5.	juhu	juu	juhu	*__________
6.	pida	piθa	pita	*__________
7.	kadi	kaθi	kati	*__________
8.	kwazi	kwasi	kwaʃi	*__________

Summary of Sound Changes:

Lang A	
Lang B	
Lang C	

Reminder … Always look for a plausible sound change first.
Only use majority rules as a last resort.

GROUP FIVE

	Lang A	Lang B	Lang C	Lang D	Proto-Form
1.	puxə	buga	pukka	puk	* ________
2.	lirə	liza	litsu	wis	* ________
3.	mani	mani	mãnni	mã	* ________
4.	wanə	jana	wãnna	wã	* ________
5.	kaxə	gaga	kakka	kak	* ________
6.	tupi	dubi	tubi	tup	* ________
7.	samu	samu	sãmmu	sã	* ________
8.	matu	madu	madu	mat	* ________

Summary of Sound Changes:

Lang A	
Lang B	
Lang C	
Lang D	

Now try this one!

Proto-Middle Indic (Note: the data has been modified)

	Magadhi Prakrit	Pali Prakrit	Maharastri	Gloss
1.	[abala]	[apara]	[avara]	other
2.	[diba]	[dipa]	[diva]	lamp
3.	[hasta]	[hatta]	[hatta]	hand
4.	[loga]	[loka]	[loa]	world
5.	[nala]	[nara]	[nara]	man
6.	[nisp^{h}ala]	[nipp^{h}ala]	[nipp^{h}ala]	fruitless
7.	[pask^{h}aladi]	[pakk^{h}alati]	[pakk^{h}alai]	(he) stumbles
8.	[pidi]	[pita]	[pia]	father
9.	[puspa]	[puppa]	[puppa]	flower
10.	[ʃuska]	[sukka]	[sukka]	dry

Proto-forms:

1.	6.
2.	7.
3.	8.
4.	9.
5.	10.

Sound Changes:

Magadhi Prakrit	Pali Prakrit	Maharastri

Try This! For each bolded sound in the reconstructed Proto-Indo-European (PIE) word, give the sound change that occurred as a result of Grimm's Law. Then give the Modern English equivalent of the proto-form.

	PIE WORD	GERMANIC SOUND (IN IPA)	ENGLISH WORD IN REGULAR SPELLING
1.	*__g__el	______________	______ool
2.	*le__b__	______________	li______
3.	*__g__re__bh__	______________	______ra
4.	*__gh__rei__b__	______________	______ri______
5.	*__p__ulo	______________	______oul
6.	*__k__oimo	______________	______ome
7.	*swa__d__	______________	swee______

REVIEW! REVIEW! Make sure you know:

- the nature of language change
- the causes of language change (five)
- how change spreads through a language and its population
- the different types of sequential, segmental, and auditory sound changes
- how to identify sound changes
- the difference between phonological splits, mergers, and shifts
- the sound changes making up the Great Vowel Shift
- the three sound changes making up Grimm's Law
- the different types of morphological and syntactic change
- the different types of lexical and semantic change
- how to reconstruct proto-forms and summarize sound changes
- about the role of naturalness and typology in language reconstruction

QUESTIONS? PROBLEMS? DIFFICULTIES?

NOTES